EDITOR: LEE JOHNSON

 ELITE SERIES 57

THE ROYAL MARINES 1939-93

Text by
NICK VAN DER BIJL
Colour plates by
PAUL HANNON

First published in Great Britain in 1994 by
Osprey, an imprint of Reed Consumer Books Ltd.
Michelin House, 81 Fulham Road,
London SW3 6RB
and Auckland, Melbourne, Singapore and
Toronto

ISBN 1 85532 388 5

Filmset in Great Britain
Printed through Bookbuilders Ltd, Hong Kong

Author's dedication
To Penny and Imogen.

Acknowledgements
Grateful thanks to Lee Johnson and Iain MacGregor of
Reed International for their support and encourage-
ment in the production of this book.

Publisher's note
Readers may wish to study this title in conjunction with
the following Osprey publications:

MAA 65	*The Royal Navy*
MAA 112	*British Battledress 1937–61*
MAA 132	*The Malayan Campaign*
MAA 133	*Battle for the Falklands (1) Land Forces*
MAA 156	*The Royal Marines*
MAA 174	*The Korean War 1950–53*
Elite 44	*Security Forces In Northern Ireland*

Artists's note
Readers may care to note that the original paintings
from which the colour plates in this book were prepared are available for private sale. All reproduction
copyright whatsoever is retained by the publisher. All
enquiries should be addressed to:

Paul Hannon
90 Station Road,
King's Langley,
Hertfordshire,
WD4 8LB

The publishers regret that they can enter into no
correspondence upon this matter.

INTRODUCTION

On 28 October 1664, the newly-raised Duke of York and Albany's Maritime Regiment, which was also known as the Admiral's Regiment, paraded on the City of London Artillery Ground 'to be in readiness to be distributed in His Mat's Fleet prepared for sea service'. This marked the formation of the Royal Marines who served with the Royal Navy as snipers, landing parties, discouragers of mutinies, ceremonial guards and later gun turret crews and bandsmen. Two hundred and seventy-five years later, at the outbreak of the Second World War on 3 September 1939, the Royal Marine strength stood at about 15,000. However, apart from ship's detachments and aircrew with the Fleet Air Arm, the Corps contributed little in the first years of the war. In 1942, the formation of a Royal Marine 'A' Commando, which participated at Dieppe, was significant and within a year nine more Royal Marine Commandos had been raised and joined the Special Service Group. 4th Special Service Brigade which landed at D-Day was entirely Royal Marine and in Burma 3rd Commando

Brigade (3 Cdo Bde) fought the Japanese. Those not required for commando service re-mustered to the massive landing craft fleet in Europe and the Far East. Demobilisation commenced after the defeat of Japan in August 1945. The Royal Marine strength dropped from its wartime 70,000 to 13,000 and settled into three broad functions of Sea Service, Commandos and Amphibious. 3 Cdo Bde based around 40, 42 and 45 Cdos retained the green beret.

The Commandos served, usually under Army command in Palestine, Malaya and Korea. In 1952, 3 Cdo Bde moved to Malta and was assigned to the Middle East Strategic Reserve, which saw service in the Canal Zone, Cyprus, where 45 Cdo developed ski techniques, and Suez, where 45 Cdo carried out the first heliborne assault. In 1959 National Service ceased, establishment dropped to 9000 men but all members of the Royal Marines became commando trained.

In 1960 the Landing Platform Helicopter (LPH) HMS *Bulwark* embarked 42 Cdo which gave the Royal Marines a strategic role; this was tested when Iraq threatened Kuwait and the Commando was landed to reinforce the local garrison. Three more

41 RM Cdo land in Buffalos launched from an LCT at Westkapelle Gap, Walcheren, 1 November 1941. (RM Museum)

carriers were converted to LPH and participated in the confrontation with Indonesia. 45 Cdo went to Aden in 1960 and stayed seven years, 45 went to Singapore and stayed eleven. 41 and 43 Cdos remained in UK for overseas operations. In 1962 HQ 3 Cdo Bde and 40 Cdo moved to the Fleet Amphibious Base Far East in Singapore where the helicopter 3 Cdo Bde Air Squadron (3 Cdo BAS) was formed. In September 1969 41 Cdo was the first RM united to be drafted to Northern Ireland. Army Commandos joined 3 Cdo Bde as gunners, engineers, specialists and technicians.

In 1971 as part of the defence re-organisation with greater commitments to NATO, 3 Cdo Bde left the Far East and was assigned an independent role in Norway with Allied Forces Northern Europe. In 1971 the Commando Logistic Regiment (Cdo Log Regt) was formed. Operations in Northern Ireland delayed deployment to Norway, but in 1973 the 45 Cdo Group began the first of many annual winter exercises. Royal Marine establishment was about 8000.

The launch of two Landing Platforms Dock (LPD) gave the Royal Marines an extensive amphibious capability, which proved invaluable in 1982 when 3 Cdo Bde landed on the Falkland Islands and played a major part in the defeat of the substantial Argentine garrison. The Royal Marines had a relatively minor role in the Gulf War, but played a significant part in Kurdistan in 1991.

The several Second World War amphibious raiding units eventually became the Special Boat Squadron (SBS), which is integral to the Corps. Mountain, winter and cliff assault was evolved into a Royal Marine speciality and resulted in the formation of the Mountain and Arctic Warfare Cadre (M&AW Cadre).

The Green Beret

In late 1942 No 1 (Army) Cdo had 79 different cap badges and a variety of headgear in its ranks. The officers decided on a uniform head-dress and engaged a local tam-o'-shanter firm to design a beret

Above: 26th RM Bn repair bomb damaged houses in south London, 1944–45. (RM Museum)

Marines of 45 RM Cdo display captured German flags and Nazi trophies after crossing the Wesel, March 1945. (RM Museum)

using the now familiar lovat green. When the Army Commandos were disbanded in 1946, senior Commando officers wanted the green beret to also be dropped, however Lord Louis Mountbatten insisted this distinctive head-dress should be awarded to those who had passed the commando course and were serving with the Royal Marines. Lovat green is now accepted as the formal head-dress for most amphibious troops, an exception being the Soviet Naval Infantry who wear black berets. Individual cap badges continue to be worn.

Why an Elite?

What distinguishes the Royal Marines from the French Fusilier Marines, the US Marine Corps and the Soviet, now Russian, *Morskaya Pekhota* (Naval Infantry)? One word – Commandos. This role, which they inherited from World War II Army commandos, have ensured they have a distinctive role, and organisation, within the British Armed Forces. They are the one formation that is trained to be delivered to battle by helicopter, or landing craft from ships, perhaps to spearhead a landing or to carry out a raid. Their strategic role demands the Royal Marines must be familiar with all types of terrain ranging from amphibious operations to jungle, desert and arctic warfare. In 1982, a veteran Norwegian major who fought throughout the 1940 Norwegian campaign and witnessed French, Soviet, German and Austrian mountain troops, described the Royal Marines as the best. However, unlike the Army, Royal Marines are not trained in the intricacies of armoured and mechanised warfare. They may be required to mount rapid-response deployments or fight as conventional troops in campaigns suitable for their role and organisation, although it is important to acknowledge that Royal Marines rarely operate in isolation. Their methods demand the Royal Navy, Army and RAF provide air, artillery, engineer and technical support to ensure that 3 Cdo Bde is a self-supporting formation.

The Royal Marines set themselves high standards in the selection of those who wish to serve with them. Those that wear the green beret do so in the knowledge they were selected members of an elite. Royal Marine officers and other ranks undergo identical training at the Commando Training Centre (CTC) at Lympstone, although timings set for offi-

Marine W.K. Lawlor hoists B Troop, 45 RM Cdo's 'Bash on Regardless' flag in Osnabruck, 4 April 1945. (RM Museum)

cers are more rigorous. Inheriting the World War Two army commando philosophy evolved at the commando training centre at Achnacarry, CTC is a 'microcosm of war' and teaches basic and some advanced military skills; including company support weapons, section and troop communication. The course tests stamina and strength and emphasises teamwork.

After the Royal Marine has been awarded his green beret, he must then select his Specialist Qualification (SQ). The options are wide and varied: sniper, air defence, divers, mechanics, signallers, writers, illustrators, small boat and landing craft crews, and pilots. For many Royal Marines, attendance at SQ courses will be their first exposure to other elements of the Armed Forces. They will recognise him to be a Royal Marine. When he has accrued sufficient experience, he may choose to 'go

Summary of Royal Marine Units 1939–45

BRIGADES	DURATION	SERVICE HISTORY
RM BDE	(Converted to 101 RM Bde 1940)	
1 RM Bn	1939–40	
2 RM Bn	1939–40	
3 RM Bn	1939–40	
5 RM Bn	1939–40	
101 BDE		
1 RM Bn	1940–43	Dakar: Converted to 42 (RM) Cdo/42 Cdo.
2 RM Bn	1939–40	Iceland & Dakar: Converted to 43 (RM) Cdo/43 Cdo.
3 RM Bn	1939–32	Dakar: Converted to 44 (RM) Cdo/40 Cdo.
102 RM BDE	1940–43	DAKAR: HQ CONVERTED TO HQ 3 SS BDE/3 CDO BDE RM
2 RM Bn	1939–43	Iceland & Dakar: Converted to 43 (RM) Cdo/43 Cdo.
3 RM Bn	1939–43	Dakar: Converted to 44 (RM) Cdo/40 Cdo.
5 RM Bn	1940–43	Dakar: Converted to 45 (RM) Cdo/45 Cdo.
RM DIV	1940–43	TRAINING & AMPHIBIOUS EXPERIMENTAL FORMATION: CONVERTED TO HQ SS GROUP/ HQ CDO FORCES
15 RM Bn	1940–43	Machine gun coys RM Div & landing craft.
18 RM Bn	1940–44	Bren gun carriers & motor cycle mobile coys.
20 RM Bn	1940–42	RM Div Reinforcement Depot/Training.
21 RM Bn	1942	Holding Bn for Royal Marines who could not be posted to operational units. Merged with 20 RM Bn.
ARTY HQ RM DIV		
RM Fd Regt	1942–43	
RM A/Tank Regt	1942–43	
RM Light AA Regt		
103 RM BDE	1940–42	
8 RM Bn	1941–42	Converted to RM B Cdo & then 41 (RM) Cdo/41 (Indep) Cdo/41 Cdo.
9 RM Bn	1941–43	Converted to 46 (RM) Cdo.
10 RM Bn	1941–43	Converted to 47 (RM) Cdo.
104 RM BDE	1942–43	RM DIV TRAINING BDE
22 RM Bn	1942–44	Training Bn under 19 years old.
23 RM Bn	1943–44	Training Bn merged with 22 RM Bn to become RM Training Group Wales.
116 RM BDE	1945–46	NORTH-WEST EUROPE UNDER ARMY COMMAND
27 RM	1944–46	Raised from LC crews.
28 RM Bn	1944–46	Beach Group.
30 RM	1945–46	Raised from LC crews.
117 RM BDE	1945	OCCUPIED GERMAN bases UNDER RN COMMAND
31 RM Bn	1945	Joined 116 RM Bde to accept surrender of the German fleet.
32 & 33 RM Bn	1945	Occupied German bases.
11 RM Bn	1940–44	Land Defence Force MNBDO 1.
12 RM Bn	1942–44	Land Defence Force MNBDO 2 Mobile coys.
19 RM Bn	1940–44	Defence coy at Scapa Flow (MNBDO 1).
24 RM Bn	1943–45	MNBDO 1 in Ceylon.
26 RM Bn	1944–46	UK bomb damage repair unit.
29 RM Bn	1944–46	Formed 34 Amph Assit Regt RM.

SB' and join the Special Boat Squadron (SBS). This small Special Forces unit is an elite within an elite; a parachute trained, swimmer-canoeist, an expert in beach reconnaissance, sabotage, intelligence gathering and anti-terrorist operations. Other Royal Marines may be drafted to Commachio Group, which is tasked with protecting offshore oil rigs from attack by terrorists and hostile forces.

In terms of firepower and numbers the Royal Marines are no match to the USMC. Royal Marines chuckle when comparisons are drawn and emphasise that firstly, quantity does not equate with quality, and secondly, age before beauty. Moreover they are 'Royals' while the USMC are Marines.

ROYAL MARINE UNITS

The MNBDOs

The 1920 *Madden Report* suggested the creation of a Royal Marine infantry brigade to defend bases and anchorages seized by the Royal Navy. Amphibious techniques to identify tide states, beach composition and shore logistics were deemed essential but unfortunately available funds allowed only for limited development. The Army had forgotten most lessons learnt at the 1915 Gallipoli landings and thus when the Second World War broke out, the limited amount of amphibious experience entirely rested with the Royal Marines. In 1939, the Hostilities Only (HOs) Royal Marines joined the military formations and were drafted to either the MNBDO, nicknamed by some as 'Men Not To Be Posted Overseas', or the Royal Marine Brigade (RM Bde).

MNBDO 1 was formed in UK in September 1939 and from 12 April–27 May 1940 provided Faroes Force, which occupied the Faroes against unenthusiastic Danish objections. By December MNBDO 1 had expanded into a 4500-strong unit divided into an Air Defence, which was employed in home defence operations during the Battle of Britain and subsequent Blitz, a Land Defence, a Coast Defence and a Landing and Maintenance Group. In March 1941, MNBDO 1 deployed to the Middle East expecting to be employed with the Mediterranean Fleet. However, in May elements were sent to Crete to reinforce the Army. During the German 7 Parachute Division's (7 Para Div) parachute and glider attack, its two 2 RM AA Regt batteries retired in good order after Maleme airfield was captured on 20 May. 11 RM Searchlight Bn fought as infantry and 1 RM Coast Bde helped Australians defend the evacuation areas at Suda-Canea and Heraklion, which allowed the 18,000 British, Australian and New Zealanders to escape. MNBDO 1 lost twelve hundred men, mostly captured. Two LC Coy/MNBDO 1 boats were sailed under jury rigs to North Africa by evading soldiers and included Royal Marines.

Tobruk

The Landing Defence Force/MNBDO 1, 11 RM Bn, was practised in amphibious landings and on 15

Marine Naval Base Defence Organisation

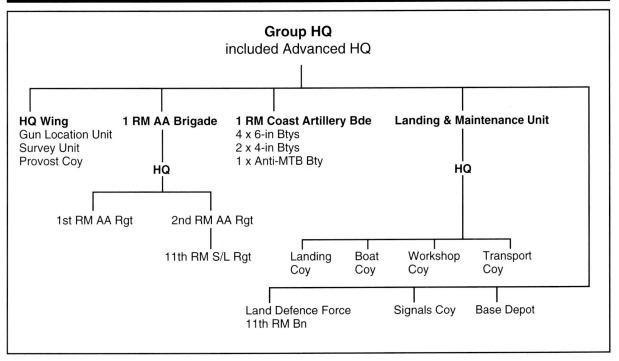

Guards from 27th RM Bn on board a surrendered German U-Boat at *Wilhelmshaven, 1945. (RM Museum)*

April 1942, elements rowed ashore and raided a radar site on Crete. On 14 September 1942, the Battalion was nominated for a raid on the much-contested port of Tobruk to destroy enemy installations and release prisoners of war. Unfortunately, the planning was complicated, rehearsals too few, and security non-existent. Elements of the Middle East Commando, the Long Range Desert Group (LRDG) and the covert Special Identification Group, entered Tobruk from the desert without arousing suspicion, but the cross-decking from destroyers by inexperienced Army and Royal Marines was chaotic. The flimsy wooden LCAs were unreliable, the troops heavily laden and the sea choppy. The destroyers then re-tired out of range and returned later expecting to disembark the second assault waves into empty LCAs, but found instead several broken down and waterlogged ones, some still loaded with Royal Marines. As HMS *Sikh* manoeuvred to recover the wet and cold men, she came under intense fire which eventually sank her. Several landing craft did make the shore, although some were smashed on rocks. Two Royal Marine platoons and some Army units assembled on the beaches east of Tobruk and during

Royal Marines of 3 Cdo Bde jungle training in Ceylon. (RM Museum)

a bid to reach the desert lost more men eliminating enemy positions; they also had the misfortune to shoot up a tented military hospital before they realised its actual use. The survivors sheltered in caves used by the Australians in 1941 but were captured the following day. Raids the same night by the Special Air Service (SAS) on Benghazi were defeated, although the LRDG successfully raided Barce.

Force 'Viper'

106 volunteers from the 1st RM Coast Regt/ MNBDO 1 joined some Burma Naval Volunteer Reserves and civilian engineers in Rangoon in February 1942 and formed Force 'Viper', named after the only British snake to have a nasty bite. Their first job was to patrol Rangoon port, using Irrawaddy Flotilla Company boats. General William Slim's Burma Corps left Rangoon on 6 March on the long retreat to India. The left flank along the Irrawaddy and Chindwin rivers was protected by Force 'Viper', who soon became adept at demolition, improvising the building of booms, and ambushing Japanese river patrols. Reinforced by Burma Commando II, the

Royal Marines and Army Commandos from the Royal West Kent Regt making up charges, Burma 1943. (RM Museum)

force attacked Japanese positions at Henzada on 17 March but on 26 March was ambushed at Padaung, losing several men; replacements were drafted from the Army's Inland Water Companies. Toward the end of the retreat the surviving Royal Marines and the remnants of 1 Gloucesters formed a rearguard at Monya, but were too few to delay the Japanese 215 Regt from capturing the vital town. On 30 April Force 'Viper' sank their boats across the Irrawaddy and the 48 survivors walked into India. MNBDO 1 remained in the Far East until 1944 when it was disbanded on its return to UK, although its 1 and 2 RM AA Bde transferred to 5 AA Bde.

MNBDO 2 was formed in January 1941 from elements of MNBDO 1 in UK. They also were actively involved in air Home Defence until 1943 when the unit was drafted to the Middle East, where units were detached to serve with 8th Army. Its 3 RM(Heavy) and 4(Light) AA Regts defended Augusta port in Sicily. MNBDO 2 returned to UK in 1944 and was disbanded, its two defence units also joining 5 AA Bde.

The Royal Marine Division

The RM Bde, which was about half the size of an Army brigade, was formed in 1939 for a role that included operations against Italy in the Mediterranean. In August 1940, it expanded into 101, 102 and 103 RM Bdes to create the RM Div, which included an RM artillery brigade; it was commanded by Maj. Gen. Robert Sturges. Its deployment was difficult because it lacked sufficient combat arms and support services and there was a reluctance by the Admiralty to place it under Army command; it spent most of its existence on amphibious training. Nevertheless in September 1940, 101 and 102 RM Bdes sailed with Force 110 to Dakar to be ready to invade the Spanish Atlantic Islands in the event that Spain sided with the Axis. In 1942 104 RM(Training)Bde joined the Division but in 1943, the RM Div was disbanded, its personnel being remustered commando or landing craft. Maj.Gen. Sturges converted its HQ to HQ SS Group, when he took command of the formation. HQ 101 RM Bde was converted to HQ 4 SS Bde, the only entirely Royal Marine formation in the SS Gp.

In January 1945, many demustered Royal Marine landing craft crews transferred to 116 and 117 RM Bdes. Although intended for Far East operations, 116 RM Bde was committed to 21st Army Group command in Belgium and for several weeks had 41 and 48(RM)Cdos under command manning observation posts along the River Maas. In April, 116 RM Bde was placed under 4(Canadian)Armd Div and took part in the battle for Oldenburg; they were the first Allied troops to enter Wilhemshaven. When 117 RM Bde, which was under Royal Navy command, arrived after the German surrender, both Brigades set about accepting the surrender of the

German Navy and occupied captured ports and harbours. Other Royal Marine wartime expansions included the Royal Marine Siege Regiment, which manned huge static and railway guns that fired across the Channel.

Ships' Detachments

Traditionally the first need of the Royal Marines was to provide men for the Fleets. In 1939 senior Royal Marine officers declared their preference for naval operations by drafting recalled fully trained reservists and pensioners for Sea Service. The early policy of the Sea Service would lead to the Royal Marines seeing little action, compared to their counterparts in the Army. It was not until the formation of the Commandos in 1942 that this would change, and they could take an active role. There is some evidence that after the war, the rigours of commando service were more popular. Even in the mid-1950s, a former Royal Marine recalls astonishment when he decided to go on Sea Service. Royal Marines manned at least one main turret, usually the After X turret, and some of the secondary weapons. A band was often found on board. The entire detachment also provided sentries and the bulk of the ceremonial contingent.

Royal Marines saw extensive action in all operational theatres and were present at all the Fleet actions. None survived the sinking of HMS *Hood* (150 strong) although those on board HMS *King George V* (350 strong) had the satisfaction of witnessing the sinking of the *Bismarck*. In the Far East, survivors from HMS *Prince of Wales* and *Repulse* were formed into a Special Service Platoon and raided Japanese positions and protected demolition squads during the withdrawal to Singapore. They were then attached to the decimated 2nd Argylls as C and D Coys and were known as the 'Plymouth-Argylls'. During the Madagascar operation in May

Above: Japanese soldiers hand over their arms to Royal Marines of either 42 or 44 RM Cdos, Hong Kong, 15 September 1945. (RM Museum)

Gun detatchment of RM Siege Regt run to reload 13.5-ins railway gun which has just fired across the English Channel, 19 November 1941. (RM Museum)

1942, a fifty-strong HMS *Ramillies* (147 strong) detachment landed from the destroyer HMS *Anthony* on a key jetty, which precipitated the surrender of the Vichy French naval base of Diego Suaraez. Royal Marine gunners also manned guns on board Defensively Equipped Merchant Ships (DEMS) in the Battle of the Atlantic.

Ships' Detachments also provided shore parties. The Royal Navy spearheaded the Allied response to the German invasion of Norway and on 14 April 1940, 300 sailors and Royal Marines from two cruisers landed to defend Namsos and were relieved by the Army. On 17 April 'Primrose' Force, a battalion group of Royal Marines from ships' detachments and MNBDO 1 air defence and artillery, sailed from UK and after landing at Aadalsnes, was placed under Army command to defend the port and form the rearguard for the withdrawal of Allied forces. From 10–17 May detachments from three capital ships landed in Iceland as Force Sturges and handed over to an Army infantry brigade. The Chatham Grand Division provided several Royal Marine units to cover the withdrawal from Europe. From 12–14

Left: A commando training in cliff assault – he appears to be a member of No 6 (Polish) Troop, 10 Inter-Allied Commando, not RM. (RM Museum)

Commandos practice cliff assaults, possibly near Dundonald or at Achnacarry, c. 1943. (RM Museum)

May, 'Hook of Holland' Coy defended the port demolition parties. On 23 May 'Boulogne' Coy helped to organise the evacuation of military and civilian personnel and prepared the port for demolition. 'Calais' Coy landed on 25 May and fought with 30 Bde at Calais, losing over 50% killed, wounded and captured, including all the officers, when the formation surrendered on 27 May.

During the Korean War, the first Royal Marines in the theatre were ten Far East Fleet volunteers, known as 'Poundforce', who were attached to the US Raider Coy and took part in several raids. After the departure of 41(Indep)Cdo in December 1950, ships' detachments continued to raid north of the 38th Parallel.

In 1955, two Royal Marines from the survey ship *Vidal* abseiled onto Rockall and annexed this rocky outcrop, arguably the last time Britain claimed territory. By 1956, there were about 2000 Royal Marines on ships in about 30 detachments, such as HMS *Belfast* which had one hundred. The appearance of missile weapon systems led to the closure of the Gunnery Wing at Eastney and by 1959, with the demise of large ships and the ending of National Service, detachment establishments were reduced to a Royal Marine officer and 20. In 1965, the last major detachment was withdrawn from the aircraft-carrier HMS *Centaur* and thereafter were deployed only for specific commissions such as the 'Cod Wars' with Iceland and the restoration of order in British Guiana in 1964. In 1966, a detachment from the polar ship HMS *Protector* was involved on the Falkland Islands when enthusiastic Argentinian activists hijacked an aircraft to Stanley. Naval Party (NP) 8901 was subsequently installed in Moody Brook Barracks. By 1978, to account for less accommodation on board, ships' detachments were reduced further to a SNCO, normally known as the Detachment Sergeant Major, a JNCO and eight Royal Marines in their own barracks and commanded by a ship's officer, who is known as OC Royal Marines. In April 1982, the HMS *Endurance* expanded detachment fought the unsuccessful action at Grytviken against an Argentinian 1 Mne Inf Bn platoon and elements of the Buzo Tactico (tactical divers), during which they shot down a Puma helicopter and severely damaged the frigate *Granville* with a 66mm Light Anti Tank Weapon (LAW). With little hope of relief, the detachment surrendered. Detachments took part in the Persian Gulf Armilla Patrols in the 1980s, boarded Iraqi ships during the Gulf War and inspected French trawlers off the Channel Islands in 1993.

Detachments are all commando-trained and drafted for sea service as part of their normal career patterns, although volunteers are always welcome. Draftees undergo seamanship courses before joining their ships. Their role is to provide helicopter and boat boarding parties, watchkeeping and manning secondary weapon systems.

Naval Parties

The Royal Marines had a significant role in manning shore-based Naval Parties (NP). These included the 1500 series which from 1944–45 provided Port Parties and Beach 'Bricks' in Europe to clear obstructions, carry out bomb disposal, provide boats' crews and salvage equipment. NP 2512 had a Royal Marine

landing-craft flotilla to support the testing of H-bombs on Christmas Island and in 1982 NP 8901 was forced to surrender to the Argentinian Amph Cdo Coy when it unsuccessfully defended Stanley. It returned with 3 Cdo Bde as J Coy 42 Cdo (J/42 Cdo) and took part in the battle for Mt Harriet.

The Royal Marine Commandos

During the Norwegian campaign, the War Office needed an amphibious striking force to harry the German coastal flank. Although the MNBDO and the RM Bde were the ideal choice, the Admiralty would not release them. The Army's Military Intelligence (Research) seized the initiative and formed ten Independent Companies (Indep Coys) from Territorial Army Divisions. Soon after Dunkirk, Prime Minister Winston Churchill issued a directive 'to organise small self-contained, thoroughly-equipped raiding units' to '. . . strike terror down the enemy coast (of Europe)'. This led to the first raid by No 11 Indep Coy against occupied France on 25 June 1940. Meanwhile the Army were in the process of raising ten Commandos to complement the Indep Coys and on 15 July, No 11 Indep Coy and No 3 (Army)

Commando (No 3 Cdo) raided Guernsey Island. Gen. Sir Alan Bourne RM was appointed the first Director Combined Operations to co-ordinate irregular operations. Although the Commandos were primarily Army, Royal Marines did join No 8 Cdo as individuals. In November, these forces were grouped into the SS Bde of five SS battalions. They quickly established themselves as the spearhead unit and evolved raiding techniques, skills and equipments using increasingly larger unit strengths.

In 1941, Lord Louis Mountbatten was appointed as Chief Combined Operations and identified the need for more Commandos to replace several Army Commandos which had been disbanded after being mauled in Crete. HQ Home Forces however opposed the raising of more Commandos, claiming that divisions were needed to be trained for the invasion of Europe. Despite objections from within Royal Marines that the Corps was more suited to serving the Fleet and on coastal batteries, Mountbatten persuaded the Admiralty to authorise the raising of the Royal Marine Commando (RM Cdo) from the RM Div to serve alongside the Army Commandos. The volunteers assembled at Deal North Barracks on 14 February 1942 well aware they would have to fight not only the enemy but also for the right to call themselves Commandos. The Achnacarry commando course was not yet mandatory for the Royal Marines but the 250 who volunteered were survivors of a rigorous weeding process. Commanded by Lt.Col. Joseph Picton-Phillips RM, the unit moved into billets on the Isle of Wight and was renamed Royal Marine 'A' Commando (RM 'A' Cdo).

Dieppe

By 1942, the invasion of Europe had become a top priority for Combined Operations. Although the aim of the Dieppe attack has never really been stated, the lessons learnt proved invaluable for D-Day two years later. The attacking force was the 2(Canadian)Div, 1st US Ranger Battalion (1 US Rangers) and four Commandos including RM 'A' Cdo. Armour, engineers, offshore fire support and fighter ground attack were available. Although the below-strength 302 Inf Div defended the Dieppe sector, the element of surprise was lost when the convoy encountered a small German patrol. Nevertheless early on 19 August, the assault forces landed across eight beaches in and around Dieppe. The Canadian battalions immediately suffered casualties and reports gave no clear idea of the situation. Originally assigned to cut out coastal craft and barges in Dieppe harbour, the 17 officers and 350 other ranks of RM 'A' Cdo received instructions 'to support the Canadian Royal Highland Light Infantry on WHITE beach, skirt the town and attack gun batteries on the east cliff', a distance of two and a half miles, over ground which no-one had yet advanced twenty yards. RM 'A' Cdo transferred to landing craft and as the Commando neared the beaches, Lt.Col. Picton-Phillips saw the appalling situation on the beaches; pulling on white gloves, he successfully signalled the second wave to go about but was then killed. His LCM and two LCAs beached and most of the Royal Marines took cover behind abandoned Calgary Regiment Churchill tanks where most were killed or captured. Some Royal Marines from sunken landing craft swam to

Left: A young officer in training in command of marines embarked on an LCA at the Amphibious School RM, Poole, c. 1960. (RM Museum)

Marines practice landing from a Dory, c. 1950s. (RM Museum)

Royal Marines prepare to land from an LCP (also known as R-boat, Eureka boat, or Higgins boat) during training in the 1950s. (RM Museum)

the beach, while others were rescued two or three miles out to sea. 76 RM 'A' Cdo failed to make roll call, but those that survived owed much to the gallantry of Lt.Col. Picton-Phillips. Valuable lessons were learnt, not the least of which was swimming as a means of survival, which now forms an essential element of training. Canadian losses were grievous.

In August 1942, RM 'A' Cdo was renamed 40 (Royal Marines) Commando (40(RM)Cdo). In October 1942 8 RM Bn was converted to RM 'B' Cdo, and underwent a weeding-out programme that reduced the 1000-strong unit to about 450 and was renamed 41(RM)Cdo. Both units joined the SS Bde.

By May 1943, the SS Bde prepared for its role in the Allied offensive strategy to defeat the Axis. Its Advanced HQ of Nos 2, 3, 40 and 41 (RM) Cdos departed for the Mediterranean theatre. The remaining Commandos that were all from the Army, and other specialist raiding units, including the RMBPD, were grouped into Rear HQ, which was based in the UK. The War Office calculated that for the invasion of Europe, nine Army Commandos would be required to support the assaulting divisions, and added to this an SS brigade was also needed for operations in the Far East. However, with the departure of Advanced HQ, and HQ Home Forces still objecting to raising more from their divisions, there was a shortfall of at least three Commandos. Mountbatten again proposed to the Admiralty the Royal Marines could fill the void. In July, the Chiefs of Staff authorised the disbandment of the RM Div and

MNBDO infantry elements and on 1 August 1943, six RM battalions were converted:

    1 RM Bn to 42(RM)Cdo,
    2 RM Bn to 43(RM)Cdo,
    3 RM Bn to 44(RM)Cdo,
    5 RM Bn to 45(RM)Cdo,
    9 RM Bn to 46(RM)Cdo,
    10 RM Bn to 47(RM)Cdo.

The commando course became mandatory for the Royal Marines and 43(RM)Cdo went to Achnacarry on 7 August, which entitled those who passed the course to wear the green beret which is now so closely associated with the Corps. Those not required for commando duty were drafted to the landing-craft fleet.

Maj.Gen. Robert Sturgess, appointed by Mountbatten to command the SS Group, converted the RM Div into HQ SS Gp to join the two Army and two Royal Marine Special Service brigades which would be committed to foreign theatres of war and the invasion of Europe respectively. But this order of battle did not remain for long due to the Army Commandos resenting the conscripted Royal Marine battalions being converted to a role developed by Army volunteers. The Army believed they had enhanced the raiding tradition and that the Royal Marines were now attempting to usurp their role. The latter argued that raiding from the sea had traditionally been their area of operations and the Army Commandos were gifted amateurs. Sturgess recognised that the inter-service rivalry had to be dealt with, and by the end of 1943 the four Special Service Brigades emerged thus:

    1 SS Bde – Nos 3, 4, 6 and 44(RM)Cdos for the European theatre.
    2 SS Bde – Nos 2, 9, 40 and 43(RM)Cdo for the Mediterranean theatre.
    3 SS Bde – Nos 1, 5, 42 and 44(RM)Cdo for the Far East.
    4 SS Bde – No 10(Inter-Allied), 41, 46 and 47(RM)Cdo for the European theatre.

This was a Royal Marine formation and was initially commanded by Brig. 'Jumbo' Leicester. RM No 10(Inter-Allied)Cdo consisted of troops from countries overrun by the Axis, such as Belgium and the Netherlands.

Although most combat and service support was available through the Army, several Royal Marine specialist units were formed, for instance, the RM Engineer Commando Company (RM Engr Cdo Coy) expanded into a Commando (RM Engr Cdo). In February 1944, 71 commando sappers joined the Landing Craft Obstruction Clearance Unit (LCOCU), who were swimmers trained to clear floating obstructions. The Royal Marine Armoured Support Group (RMASG) was also formed and consisted of 1 and 2 RM Support Regts. Following the Royal Marine artillery tradition, each regiment consisted of two batteries of four troops each with one Sherman and four 95mm Centaurs. In March 1944 7 RM Bn was summoned to UK from Italy and, much to their surprise, formed into 48(RM)Cdo and slotted into 4 SS Bde. 7 RM Bn had been raised in 1941, been sent on garrison duties to South Africa and went to Egypt as No 31 Beach Brick. It took part in the invasion of Sicily and was then hurriedly committed to support the 51(Highland)Div against the Herman Goering Div from which it gained an unwarranted poor reputation.

Raiding and Special Forces

Raiding Forces

Throughout the war, most cross-Channel small-scale raiding was carried out by RN special units and Army Commandos, although there is some evidence that individual Royal Marines were involved. In May 1944, Cpl. King participated in the No 10 (Inter-Allied) Cdo Op 'Tarbrush 10' recce of the invasion beaches.

In October 1942, the Royal Marine Boom Patrol Detachment (RMBPD) carried out the legendary 'Cockleshell Heroes' raid on Bordeaux harbour, the canoeists being drafted from RM Small Arms School and RM Auxiliary Bn and trained to use the collapsible Cockle Mk 2 canoe. Two crews planted limpet mines on targeted blockade runners taking war goods to Japan. The captured crews were shot under Hitler's Commando Order. In 1942, the RMBPD transferred to Raiding Forces Middle East where several detachments parachuted on to Aegean and Adriatic islands to coastwatch. In June 1944, its 'Earthworm' Section entered Porto Lago naval base on Leros and

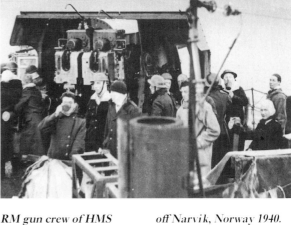

RM gun crew of HMS Cairo's twin 4-ins guns,   *off Narvik, Norway 1940. (RM Museum)*

placed limpets on several Axis ships. The RMBPD was prominent in developing small raiding craft.

In 1944 in the Far East, Lt.Col. 'Blondie' Hasler, Norway landing craft and Cockleshell leader, formed the Special Operations Group (SOG), which included Royal Marine Detachment 385 (RM Det 385). Operational by January 1945, its first raid was disastrous but subsequent operations were successful and included raiding the coast of Thailand and recovering parties operating behind Japanese lines. It perfected a technique of launching canoes from flying boats. Group X was an Australia-based canoe raiding unit that first penetrated Singapore in October 1943. Returning a year later, all were captured and executed including Royal Marine Maj. M.J. Ingleton.

Operations room of the RM Siege Regt, Lt.Col. L.L. Foster   *standing over the plotting table with his stop watch. (RM Museum)*

The Special Boat Squadron

At the cessation of hostilities, the newly-established Amphibious School Royal Marines included the Small Raids and Small Boat Wings from the swimmer–canoeist Combined Operations Beach and Boat Section (COBBS), RM Det 385 and RMBPD. Swimmer–canoeists operated in the Malayan Emergency and in Korea Poundforce helped to survey the Inchon beaches for the 1(US)Mne Div landings. In 1951 Special Boat (SB) Sects were formed for European operations. In 1957, the Small Raids/Small Boat Wing was renamed the SB Unit and the following year SB Coy. During Confrontation, SB Sects operated closely with 3 Cdo Bde and Army units and took part in operations to intercept, ambush and harry Indonesian Army patrols attempting to penetrate the states. On occasion teams crossed the border to disrupt Indonesian infiltration. In 1975, SB Coy was retitled the Special Boat Squadron (SBS) and thus assumed the initials of the wartime SAS Special Boat Section; the SAS have retained their Boat Troops. In the Falklands campaign, the SBS were involved in operations to recapture South Georgia, landed on the Falklands to gather intelligence, captured an Argentinian surveillance ship and neutralised an enemy OP during the San Carlos landings. Operating ahead of 3 Cdo Bde, the SBS lost an NCO killed in a 'blue on blue' with the SAS. During the 1991 Gulf War, the SBS carried out several operations with Allied Special Forces behind the Iraqi lines.

The SBS is administered by HQ Training, Reserve and Special Forces. Much of their work is of a classified nature but includes intelligence-gathering, sabotage, navigation marking for amphibious forces, recce and counter-terrorism; they remain very closely integrated with their Corps. Entry is open to Royal Marines, who must pass the rigorous Swimmer/Canoeist III selection course. The traditional craft now used is the Klepper Mk 2 canoe; the Mk 13 is collapsible.

Mountain and Arctic Warfare

Cliff assault has always been prominent in Royal Marine Commando operations; on D-Day, 46(RM)Cdo was held in readiness for a cliff assault. The Army's Commando Mountain and Snow Warfare Training Camp with Norwegian Tp Nos 10(Inter-Allied), 12 and 14 Cdos pioneered winter warfare

Above: Troops embark from an LCA onto a destroyer following the Dieppe raid.
(RM Museum)

Royal Marines of Force Viper on the Irawaddy river – launch 'Stella', February 1942.
(RM Museum)

techniques for operations in occupied Norway; its successors are the SAS Mountain Tps. The Royal Marine Cliff Assault Wing (CAW) trained troops to get off beaches situated next to high cliffs. In the 1950s, 42 Cdo made further cold weather developments although the clothing was considerably inferior to that issued today. In 1962, the CAW became the Cliff Assault Troop, which in 1965 became the Recce Leader troop from which the Mountain and Arctic Warfare Cadre Royal Marines (M&AW Cadre) was formed in 1970. Operating in teams of about four, the unit is 3 Cdo Bde's speciality recce troops; on the Northern Flank they tend to work above the tree line. In 1982, a M&AW Cadre section defeated an Argentinian 602 Cdo Coy section at Top Malo House. All entrants must pass the tough Mountain Leader 3 (ML 3) course. After a tour, MLs are usually drafted to a Commando Recce Troop.

Raiding Squadrons

1 RSRM is one of two small boat units attached to 3 Cdo Bde HQ and Signal Sqn, the other being 2 RSRM (V). In 1980 3 RSRM was raised specifically for anti-illegal immigrants operations in Hong Kong and was disbanded in 1988. Currently equipped with Dell Quay Rigid Raiders and Avon Gemini, the RSRM role is to provide a fast inshore capability for small patrols and raiding parties for all units within the Brigade.

Comacchio Group

In July 1977, L/42 Cdo took part in the 'Oil Safe' programme to protect Britain's offshore oil reserves against attack. In 1980, Comacchio Coy Royal Marines (named after the action in which Cpl Tom Hunter won the VC) was formed with the specific role of responding to military action against oil rigs. There are now two components namely P Coy, which has a RN nuclear escort role, and O Coy for oil-rig protection: Both company designations originated from 43 Cdo. The organisation is now known as Comacchio Group and is based at Arbroath in close proximity to the North Sea oilfields, though details of their operations are not widely known.

Air

Fixed Wing

During the Second World War, Royal Marine pilots served with the Fleet Air Arm (FAA). During the Norwegian campaign, Capt. R.J. Partridge, CO the Skua equipped 803 NAS, led the attack which sank the cruiser *Konisberg* in Bergen. Three Royal Marine pilots are believed to have fought in the Battle of Britain while others flew with Coastal Command. Capt. Oliver Patch, flying a Swordfish torpedo-bomber, participated in the famous Taranto attack on 11 November 1940 which shattered the Italian Fleet. 821 NAS Albacores commanded by Maj. Alan Newson became adept at pathfinding in the Western

9 (Army) Commando aboard a motor launch in the Adriatic, 9 August 1944. (RM Museum)

45 RM Cdo leave their camp near Horndean to embark at Warsash for the passage to Normandy. (RM Museum)

Desert and later helped defend Malta while Capt. R.C. Hay led a Fulmar-equipped Army Co-operation unit in the Italian theatre. In the Far East, Royal Marine aircrew flying Avengers and Corsairs from aircraft-carriers operating in the Sumatra Sea, and then with the British Pacific Fleet attached to the US Sixth Fleet, were prominent in raiding Japanese installations. After the war, Royal Marines continued flying fixed-wing aircraft until training ceased in 1959.

Support Helicopters

During the 1956 Suez landings, 45 Cdo, some REs and RAF carried out the first helicopter assault on enemy positions. At 08.00 on 6 November 1956 ten 845 NAS Whirlwinds on the aircraft-carrier HMS *Ocean* and six Experimental Helicopter Unit Whirlwinds and six Sycamores on HMS *Theseus* lifted the 415-strong 45 Cdo and 22 tons of stores in four waves in 90 minutes to a secondary LZ near the de Lesseps statue. Several aircraft were damaged by ground fire including one Whirlwind carrying wounded forced to ditch. This action began a very close association between the Royal Marines and the FAA support helicopter units and by 1961 Royal Marines were flying helicopters. In 1962, 845 and 846 NAS, equipped with Wessex Mk7s and Whirlwind Mk7s, supported 3 Cdo Bde operations from the commando carriers in Confrontation. The two Commando Heli-

copter Support Squadrons proved their value in Aden, the evacuation of British and Commonwealth citizens from Cyprus in 1974 and UN operations in the Gulf and Bosnia. During the Falklands campaign, 845, 846, 847 and 848 NAS supported land operations, although D/848 NAS lost its aircraft when the *Atlantic Conveyor* was sunk. 845 and 846 NAS are now equipped with the Sea King HC Mk 4 support helicopters, popularly known as Sea Junglies, which have a lift of twenty-eight troops.

Light Helicopters

In 1963, 40(Dieppe) and 42(Kangaw) Air Tps were formed to support the Commando Recce Troops, as was 29(Brunei) Air Tp to provide air observation for 29 Cdo Light Regt RA. A close relationship soon evolved with the Army Air Corps (AAC). As part of the 3 Cdo Bde rationalisation for independent operations, 3 Commando Brigade Air Squadron (3 Cdo BAS) was formed in Singapore in 1968 from an amalgamation of the existing Commando Air Troops. It was then equipped with Agusta-Bell Sioux AH 1 helicopters and had, and still has, a standard role of a light helicopter unit to provide liaison, casevac, recce, a small troop taxi service and anti-tank support. Two years later 41(Salerno) and 45(Montforterbeck) Air Tps were absorbed into the Squadron. In 1970, four Westland Scouts were introduced to give a combined SS-11 anti-tank and

48 RM Cdo advance from St Aubin-sur-Mer to Langrune, D-Day 1944. Most are wearing green berets under their steel helmets. (RM Museum)

casevac capability. After returning from the Far East, 3 Cdo BAS spent several years in Plymouth and in 1975 was re-equipped with 12 Aerospatiale SA341 Gazelles AH 1 to replace the Sioux. During the Falklands campaign, 3 Cdo BAS was reinforced by S/656 Sqn AAC. The Scouts and Gazelles proved most valuable although several were lost, including two Gazelles shot down by a retreating Argentinian combat team on 21 May at Port San Carlos; two Scouts were lost during the Battle of Goose Green and a 656 Sqn Gazelle was mistakenly shot down by a British ship. In 1983, already the largest light helicopter unit in the Armed Forces, 3 Cdo BAS moved to Royal Naval Air Station Yeovilton. The Scouts have been replaced by six Westland Lynx AH 1 fitted with TOW anti-tank missile variants. The two Gazelle flights of four aircraft principal role is recce in support of the Lynx anti-armour operations. M Flt is

absorbed into the 45 Cdo Gp. HQ Flt is responsible for the daily management of the Squadron and a fifth flight provides all aspects of ground support. REME personnel maintain and repair the aircraft. The organisation is geared solely to provide anti-tank and recce support to 3 Cdo Bde, which includes operations from many types of warship and merchantmen.

Air Operations

Ground control for all helicopter operations is through the Commando Helicopter Operations and Support Cell (CHOSC) controlling RN and RM Mobile Air Operation Teams (MAOTs). The Tacti-

3-ins mortar of 7th RM Bn, Sicily, 21 July 1943. (RM Museum)

cal Air Control Parties (TACP) 605, 611 and 612 Sects provide forward air control for close air support. Generally consisting of Royal Marines but the TACPs have included commando-trained RAF. The teams are administered by 3 Cdo Bde HQ and Signal Sqn.

Air defence

The MNBDOs

Both MNBDOs had an Air Defence Bde, which consisted of two Anti-Aircraft Regts and a Searchlight Regt. MNBDO 1 were involved in Home Defence during the Battle of Britain and the Blitz and then in early 1941 departed for the Middle East where 'C' Bty and 23 LAA Tp took part in the battle for Crete. In 1941, it was deployed to the Far East. In 1943, MNBDO 2 moved to Italy, where its 3 RM(Heavy) and 4(Light)AA Regts served with 8th Army and defended Augusta port in Sicily. Both MNBDOs were disbanded in 1944, their air defence units joining 5 AA Bde.

5 AA Bde

5 AA Bde was formed in March 1944 and during the defence of southern England was credited with one hundred and twenty V-1 rockets. In September, it assumed responsibility for the defence of the Scheldt estuary and had several Army AA units under command. Its 1, 2, and 3 RM(Heavy)Regts 3.7" howitzers often fired in the ground support role.

AD Tp

On the disbandment of 5 AA Bde in April 1945, the Royal Marines' direct association with air defence ceased until the late 1970s when the Air Defence Tp 3 Cdo Bde HQ and Signal Sqn was formed to protect 3 Cdo Bde units. Equipped with Shorts Blowpipe with the shoulder-launched surface to air missile (SAM), it is credited with one Argentinian 1 Attack Sqn Navy MB-339 shot down during the Battle of Goose Green in 1982. In the mid-1980s, sections were also deployed on British merchant ships in the Persian Gulf to deter Iranian attacks. The Troop is now equipped with the Shorts Javelin surface to air missile. To supplement this light air defence, Army AD units are attached to 3 Cdo Bde, such as the Rapier-equipped T (Shah Shujah's) Bty, 12 AD Regt in the Falklands campaign.

Artillery

Although the Royal Marines had a long tradition in artillery, during the Second World War this was largely confined to the provision of coastal and air defence by the MNBDOs. In 1940, 41 RM Quick Firing Regt, equipped with 12pdrs, was formed for a short time to support 'Boulogne' and 'Calais' Coys but did not land. The RM Div Artillery Bde consisted of a field regiment, an anti-tank regiment and a light AA regiment. 102 RM Bde also formed the RM Fd Arty Regt, which was sub-divided into a battery of 3.7" howitzers, a battery of Oerlikons and Bofors AA guns, a battery of 2pdr anti-tank guns, which were replaced by 6pdr and a field artillery battery of 18pdrs. The Brigade also formed the RM Anti-Tank Regt between 1942–43, which was a four-gun battery equipped with 2 and 6pdrs anti-tank guns and 3.7" howitzers. Otherwise the Royal Marines were reliant upon the Army to provide artillery support.

Trainee marines on an LCA in Poole harbour, *probably in the early 1960s. (RM Museum)*

Royal Marines and members of 1st US Marine Corps land from an LCVP on the Shetland Islands, Exercise Northern Wedding, August 1978. (RM Museum)

In 1962 Army commandos reappeared when 29 Regt RA was converted into commando gunners. Equipped with the Italian 105mm Pack Howitzer, it soon developed into a flexible unit that can deploy anywhere in support of 3 Cdo Bde. 29 Cdo Light Regt RA then consisted of 7(Sphinx)Cdo Bty, which is now with the 45 Cdo Gp; 8(Alma)Cdo Bty, which is known as Black Eight; 79(Kirkee)Cdo Bty and 145(Maiwand)Cdo Bty, the latter soon in action in Borneo. In 1963, 95 Cdo Light Regt RA with its forward observation expertise joined 3 Cdo Bde. 29(Brunei) Air Tp was formed to provide air observation for 29 Cdo Light Regt RA and joined 3 Cdo BAS. In September 1965, 95 Cdo Light Regt deployed to the Far East, relieving 29 Cdo Light Regt, which deployed detachments to the Radfan, where the gunners taught themselves mule-packing the Pack Howitzers. In 1968 except for 148(Meiktila)Bty, which was converted into forward observation, 95 Cdo Light Regt RA was disbanded although by 1977, 289 Cdo Bty RA(V) joined 29 Cdo Regt, which in 1980 re-organised into three batteries, losing 145(Maiwand)Cdo Bty, and was re-equipped with the 105mm Light Gun. Two years later, the Regiment played a significant role in the Falklands campaign.

Forward Observation

Part of the Combined Operations organisation were Army and RN Dundonald Bombardment Units, whose role was to direct naval fire support. In 1943 Carrier Borne Air Liaison Teams (CBALs) were formed also to direct naval gunfire support for the ground forces. Although the Army were in the majority, Royal Marines were evident until 1961 when the Corps felt they were unable to provide sufficient officers and the role passed entirely to the Army. The role is now taken on by 148(Meiktila)Cdo Forward Observation Bty and 3 Cdo BAS helicopters. When 95 Cdo Light Regt RA was disbanded, 198(Meiktila)Cdo Forward Observation Bty remained to provide Naval Gunfire Forward Observation teams to control naval gunfire support from the offshore gun line, call up field artillery and control strikes from the air. Highly trained on Special Forces techniques and able to work closely with the SBS, teams are numbered Forward Observation Teams (FO) and typically consist of a RA captain, a RA bombardier second-in-command, a RN radio operator, a lance bombardier and a gunner. Insertion is usually by parachute, boat or helicopter.

Amphibious Warfare

Landing Craft

From their earliest days the Royal Marines have a long association with landing craft. That association continued during the Second World War when both MNBDOs each had a LC Coy. Although some landing craft were used in Norway, most of the landings were by ships' detachments using cutters and whalers.

The major expansion occurred in 1943 when the RM Div was disbanded and about 13,000 Royal Marines not required for commando services were re-mustered to the amphibious assault training centres and then drafted to the expanding landing craft fleet; by 1944 crews numbered 49,000 servicemen. Records suggest that four LC Support (Medium), three LC(Hedgerow (mortars)), 28 LCM and 57 LCA flotillas were manned by Royal Marines. LCAs delivered first wave assault troops to the beaches and were often skippered by Royal Marine Corporal coxswains. Royal Marine also provided gun crews for the major fire support landing craft, such as the Landing Craft, Flak (LC(F)) which carried 50 anti-aircraft gunners. Royal Marines landing craft crews manned vessels at all the main landings in Sicily, Italy and Normandy, Walcheren and Arakan, notwithstanding the many raids and outflanking operations. At Walcheren 27 major fire support landing craft drew enemy fire to cover the 4 SS Bde landings. By late 1944, the need for landing craft had lessened and the crews were remustered to 116 and 117 Bdes RM. In preparation for operations in the Pacific, several Mobile Landing Craft Advanced Bases (MOLCABs) were formed in 1945 to provide minor

landing craft shore-based and maintenance facilities when operating independent of their parent ships.

In 1946 the Royal Marines established Rhine Sqn to support 1(BR)Corps river operations in West Germany until the role was handed over to 28 Amph Regt RCT in 1960. In October 1947, Amphibious Wing Royal Marines was formed at Eastney and consisted of LC, Beach Control and Small Raids Wings and the LC Obstruction Clearance and LC Recovery Units. In December 1954, the units moved to Poole and in 1980 became Royal Marines Poole with a LC Branch supported by training and technical facilities. Poole's activities are controlled by HQ Training, Reserves and Special Forces.

Amphibious Warfare

In the 1950s, the Mediterranean Amphibious Warfare Sqn was formed to support 3 Cdo Bde and Army operations, including the Suez and Kuwait crisis. The Squadron consisted of an HQ ship, LSTs(Asslt), each with a Royal Marine Assault Sqn, and LSTs, which delivered second echelon armour. The arrival of commando carriers in the 1960s and their ability to loiter below the horizon became a feature of Confrontation. The 7 Asslt Sqn RM on board HMS *Bulwark* manned four LCVP, which are still irrelevantly known as 'rubbish skips' by the Embarked Force, and formed Beach Units. With at

Left: Royal Marines practise landing from an LCA during wartime exercises in Scotland watched by King George VI. (RM Museum)

Right: An officer of 41 (Independent) Cdo RM passing a radio message during the Sorye Dong Raid, Korea, 10 April 1951. Note the American uniform, kit and M3 'Grease Gun'. (RM Museum)

Far right: Sgt. Gates of Leeds, and Cpl. Greenwood of Halifax both of 41 (Independent) Cdo RM, fire a 2-ins mortar during a raid in Korea, June 1951. (RM Museum)

least one helicopter NAS on board, the principal means of disembarkation was by helicopter. The arrival of the two LPDs saw the disbandment of the Amphibious Warfare Sqn and the decommissioning of the commando carriers although HMS *Hermes* reverted to an aircraft-carrier. The Asslt Sqns of HMS *Fearless* 4th and HMS *Intrepid* 6th crew the four LCUs and four LCVPs on each LPD and are also trained in beach assault using the Centurion-based Beach Armoured Recovery Vehicle (BARV) and Bedford Mk 4 tonne trucks that rolls out Class 40 trackway.

Largely as a result of inshore amphibious deficiencies encountered during the Falklands, 539 Asslt Sqn was formed in 1984. A specialist unit, it has developed techniques from World War II and expanded upon them, such as 'Black Pig' which involves towing a string of 'Rigid Raiders' near the objective, and 'Brown Sow' which is the concept of concealing landing craft in small bays and inlets from which to launch raids and patrols.

ORGANISATION

Logistics

Prior to 1939, the Royal Marines developed a logistic organisation to support amphibious operations which the MNBDOs expanded into Group Supply Units. This experience was not tapped until January 1943 when the luckless 7 RM Bn, on arrival in Egypt, was ordered to structure an organisation to transfer men and material for further distribution across unsecured beaches to and from landing craft of all sizes. Retitled 'No 31 Brick', the battalion, after some experimentation, found an efficient method, which became the model for future operations. The origin of the word 'Brick' is not known, but it is now widely used to denote packets of men, typically a four-man patrol.

Throughout the war the Commandos relied upon their formation HQ for the provision of stores and equipment. The introduction of the commando carriers saw no great change in logistics because resupply was available from Fleet auxiliaries. In 1971 the Cdo Log Regt was formed to support the deployment of 3 Cdo Bde with AFNORTH as a self sufficient and independent formation operating on NATO's extreme northern flank and relatively divorced from support, other than from the Norwegians. It was eleven years until the Regiment was fully tested when it proved that it could support the Brigade during the Falklands campaign. The unit consists of several squadrons.

Headquarters

The Headquarters commands the activities and deployment of the Cdo Log Regt in accordance with HQ 3 Cdo Bde orders. On deployment, elements includes a Field Record Office, a Pay Office for Army ranks, a Royal Logistic Regiment postal and courier officer and a Force Reinforcement Holding Unit for battle casualty replacements.

Medical

On the formation of the SS Bdes in 1943, each was allocated a RAMC and RN Field Ambulance for second line medical cover. The Commando used its own personnel for the provision of stretcher bearers, although each had a MO and a RAMC and RN manned RAP. Evacuation was by any means, for instance jeep ambulance in Europe, mules in Italy and Yugoslavia and men in the Far East. This system continued until Medical Sqn was formed. Medical and dentistry support is still supplied by RN medical teams from the first-line Commando RAPs to Surgical Support Teams at HQ Medical Sqn in the Brigade Maintenance Area (BMA). Casualty evacuation is organised by the Commando Forces Band.

A Royal Marine priming an anti-tank grenade before the Suez landings. (RM Museum)

Ordnance

Both MNBDOs had RN supplied Ordnance Depots, although in Italy MNBDO 2 was reinforced by RAOC, which allowed the organisation to draw off the Army rather than the Royal Navy. The RM Div did not have a dedicated ordnance organisation, although the Beach Units controlled supply and distribution when the formation landed. Until 1971, Commando echelons were reliant upon the Army for the provision of much of their ground equipment. Ordnance Sqn maintains links with the RAOC and manages the combat supplies distribution normally with at least two months stocks in reserve. In support there is a Petroleum Coy RAOC (V). Local Resource Teams locally purchase or acquire items that are not available through the Squadron.

Transport

The MNBDOs, RM Div and Second World War Commandos had a relatively small number of vehicles on establishment. In 1943, a typical Commando MT pool was 25 bicycles, one staff car, 18 5cwt, eight 15cwt, three 3 ton trucks and one water bowser. By 1944, this had risen to 60 bicycles and at least 25 15cwt trucks. Transport requirements, until the formation of Transport Sqn, was dependent on role, although the Commandos retained MT Tps. By 1980, a Commando had an average allocation of 70 wheeled and 30 Bandwagon BV 202Es oversnow vehicles. Close links with the RCT are retained.

Workshops

Both MNBDOs had a Workshop Coy/Group to maintain and repair the considerable array of artillery. The RM Div also had a Workshop Coy as did the RM Bdes. When MNBDO 2 arrived in the Middle East in 1943, a small number of REME were assigned to maintain equipment. On the formation of the SS Bdes in 1943, each was allocated a REME manned LAD to maintain the small number of vehicles, equipment and cycles, a concept that has remained. After the war, the Commandos retained their Royal Marine-manned LADs although some

Right: 45 Cdo RM on HMS Theseus await the helicopter airlift to Port Said, 6 November 1956. (RM Museum)

REME filled specialists appointments. Workshop Sqn has the major task of ensuring that 3 Cdo Bde's vehicles, weapons, electronic instruments and radios remain operational. This is particularly hazardous in Arctic conditions where sub-zero temperatures affect the operation of sophisticated equipment. The concept is to take the repair teams to the equipment in trouble, which proved its worth during the Falklands War, particularly in supporting the vehicle-bound Brigade HQ.

Communications

On the outbreak of war, the priority was to reinforce the Fleet Royal Marine signallers and to equip the RM Signals Coys, in the Royal Marine units, with experienced signallers. Tradesmen passed through the Signals Training Wing, some of whom joined the Commando Signal Sections. A Royal Marine and Royal Navy battalion-sized group, known as Party 'Funshore', landed in Normandy to man telephone exchanges and communication centres, provide despatch-riders, repair damaged German networks and provide signallers for HQ Allied Naval Forces. Commandos Signals Sections were typically 30-strong, which has remained reasonably constant to this day.

3rd Commando Brigade Headquarters and Signal Squadron Royal Marines (3 Cdo Bde HQ and Sigs Sqn) is a 300-strong unit which once ashore operates from either Land-Rovers or oversnow vehicles, the current mode being the Swedish Bandvagn 206s (BV 206). On board the LPDs, an Amphibious Operations Room is available. Manpacking is not uncommon. Administration Tp looks after the needs of the Sqn and includes a Quartermaster element, which manages the Officers Mess, known as the 'Greasy Spoon'. The Royal Navy provides a commando-trained chaplain and a medical team. Communications Tp provides secure radio, teleprinter and line upwards, downwards and sideways communications for Brigade HQ. The signallers are all Royal Marines who have attained a specialist qualification in communications, although the technicians are usually commando-trained Royal Signals. A 30 Signals Regt Satellite Communications detachment is sometimes assigned to the Brigade to provide long range rear link communications. Y(Electronic Warfare)Tp RM provides electronic warfare support. Motor Transport Tp (MT Tp) provides specialist transport, including the Swedish Bandvagn BV 206 (BV 206) oversnow tracked amphibious prime mover and passenger unit. During the Falklands campaign the skill, high standard of driving,

THESEUS

45 Cdo RM search an EOKA store cave during Operation Turkey Trot, Cyprus, November 1955. (RM Museum)

repair and maintenance by the Troop helped to minimise vehicle losses. Defence Tp provides local ground defence of the Brigade HQ. Air Defence Tp, Royal Marine Police Tp (RMP Tp), the RSRMs and the TACPs are also Brigade assets administered by the Squadron.

Intelligence

In September 1942, Director of Naval Intelligence (DNI) authorised the formation of the Special Intelligence Unit (SIU) with No 33(RM), No 34(Army) and No 36(RN)Tp. SIU is more commonly known as 30 Cdo or 30 Assault Unit, its role being to gather intelligence, and it was designed to operate with the forward troops often working closely with the Intelligence Corps' Field Security sections. No 33(RM)Tp consisted of 22 Royal Marines, most of whom were Dieppe veterans, and their training included commando and parachute training, enemy booby-trap techniques, uniform recognition, prisoner handling and safe cracking.

33(RM)Tp was present in all theatres and usually operated independently gathering information from captured facilities. In November 1943, 30 Cdo returned to UK to prepare for the Normandy landings, which was welcomed by some in the Middle East, who found the unit's unconventional methods

irksome. In 1944, 33(RM)Tp was renamed RM Wing and consisted of fifty Royal Marines. During the capture of Cherbourg, a patrol was ambushed and two survivors captured. While one Royal Marine conveyed surrender terms, the other was locked up in the garrison main baggage store, where he continued to collect intelligence. The acceptance of the surrender of the Bremen naval base in 1945 was perhaps the RM Wing's most successful operation. A 30 Cdo Royal Marines detachment was sent to the Far East but the Japanese surrender precluded operations. Subsequent activities in Singapore, Indo-China and Hong Kong eventually provided much useful information.

Post-1945, the Intelligence Corps continued the close links with 3 Cdo Bde, providing, for instance, an Intelligence Section to HQ 3 Cdo Bde in the Far East. In the late 1970s, although Intelligence was, and is, not a Specialist Qualification, the Section was replaced by Royal Marines and one commando-trained Intelligence Corps SNCO. Intelligence Sections have supported the Commandos since their inception in 1943, one of their original tasks being to find billets. The role of all Intelligence Sections is to convert information into intelligence from a variety of sources including the interrogation of prisoners of war, document translation and patrol reports.

Engineers

In March 1940, the Royal Marine Engineers (RM Engrs) was formed with technical responsibility to the Admiralty and administrative to the Royal Marines. One battalion was allocated to MNBDO 1 building Scapa Flow defences. For the invasion of Europe, Naval Port Parties were assigned a 500-strong RM Engr company, which included divers, dock and wreckage clearance and bomb disposal teams. When Cherbourg was captured on 12 September, G/RM Engrs cleared the port in seven days instead of the projected three weeks. By early 1945 with the prospect of a need for amphibious and port engineers in the Pacific theatre, a Royal Marine general was appointed to enlarge RM Engrs from 7000 to 20,000 into companies numbering 1500, although the ending of the war precluded enhancement.

The RM Engr Cdo was formed in 1943 and by 1944 consisted of an HQ and two troops. For the D-

42 Cdo Sinals Station at Kuwait airport, 2 July 1961. (RM Museum)

Day landings, 1 and 4 SS Bde were each allocated a section and LC Obstruction Clearance Units. In November 1943 a RM Engr Cdo section joined 3 SS Bde in Arakan to hack roads and tracks out of the jungle and prepare landing points in appalling conditions.

After the war, apart from the Asslt Engr Tp in each Commando, the Royal Marines were reliant upon the Army for specialist sapper support. In 1971, 59 Field Squadron RE was converted to 59 Independent Commando Engineer Squadron RE (59 Indep Cdo Sqn RE) and absorbed into the 3 Cdo Bde order of battle; attached is 131 Indep Cdo Sqn RE(V). Both units provide Recce and several Field Tps and played a prominent role in sapper tasks during the Falklands campaign.

Provost

Both the MNBDOs and the RM Div had a Provost Coy (Provo Coy) in their HQ elements. A section landed with RM 'A' Cdo at Dieppe, another served with 7 RM Bn in Italy and another landed with 4 SS Group on D-Day. Wearing the traditional red caps of British military police, they carried out the traditional duties of civil and military law enforcement, running PoW cages, traffic control and VIP escorting. The Provo Coy was disbanded after the war,

although the Commandos have always retained Regimental Police (RP) detachments. The Royal Marine Police Tp (RMP Tp) was reformed with the reorganisation of 3 Cdo Bde in the late 1960s and has continued ever since. Its role is little different to that of the wartime RM Provo Coy, although there is now a small Special Investigation Branch (SIB). The Troop retains close links with the Royal Military Police, one of whose members often serves with the Troop. The commando-trained Cpl Dean RMP was Brig. Julian Thompson's personal protection during the Falklands campaign.

OPERATIONS WWII

The Mediterranean

Sicily

In June 1943, the SS Bde Advanced HQ sailed from Liverpool and on 10 July landed with 1(Canadian)Div against very light opposition west of Punta Castellazzo. By 16 August, Sicily had fallen to the Allies and on 3 September Italy capitulated. On the same day, 40(RM)Cdo crossed the Straits of Messina and landed at Porto San Venere to spearhead 8th Army's crossing into Italy. Meanwhile 5th (US) Army landed at Salerno, a wide, sandy bay about twenty miles south of Naples.

Salerno

No 2 and 41(RM)Cdos, as the SS Bde, landed at Vietri on 8 September but during their advance to seize the important La Molina pass, encountered increasing opposition from the German 16 Pz and Hermann Goering Divs. The situation on the beachhead became desperate under persistent and accurate bombardment and it became vital to hold the pass. For the next two days in intense heat, the brigade prevented all attempts by the Germans to breach the perimeter, 41(RM)Cdo suffering heavy casualties. No 2 Cdo then scaled a cliff overlooking Vietri and linked up with the 1 and 4 US Rangers and British 46 Div and a loose beachhead perimeter was established. On 12 September No 2 Cdo drove the Germans out of La Molina pass and held it.

The brigade returned to the beachhead for rest

but within eight hours was back on La Molina pass as German pressure mounted on 46 Div. On 13 September, German units overran the forward Commando positions, but accurate fire from 71 Fd Regt RA allowed the Commandos to successfully counterattack. Both units were again relieved and the weakened 41(RM)Cdo reorganised into four Troops. But again within the day, they were recalled from rest billets to support 56(London)Div and stabilised the situation by capturing three hills overlooking Piegoletti village, but were pushed off another peak, 'The Pimple'. Although desperately tired, 41(RM)Cdo were ordered to take it. Struck by British artillery while on the Start Line, B/41(RM)Cdo did not acknowledge the order to retire and reached the summit after a speed march. The Troop was unable to hold the ridge and the following day retired with only six men still on their feet but bringing out wounded. The SS Bde held Piegoletti and the two hills until finally relieved on 15 September. Both Commandos lost 50 per cent of their strength.

Termoli

Eighth Army ordered the seizure of the small port of Termoli to pre-empt the Germans retreating from Salerno from making a stand there. No 3 Cdo, who had lost heavily in fighting in Sicily, and 40(RM)Cdo landed on 3 October and captured Termoli and were reinforced by 11 Inf Bde/78 Inf Div, which arrived overland from the south. However, 16 Pz Div and elements of 4 Para Bde made determined attempts to

Royal Marine of 45 Cdo in the Radfan, 1966. (RM Museum)

Right: 45 Cdo Recce Troop Land-Rover on patrol in the Radfan, 1964. (RM Museum)

Royal Marine Commando – Mediterranean (1943)

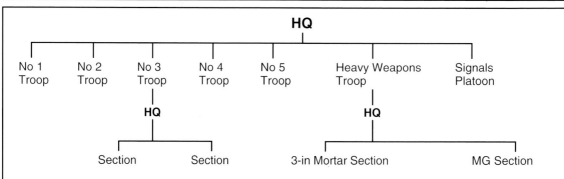

NOTES
1. Troops were named after capital ships' main and secondary gun turrets and maintained the link with the Royal Navy.
2. Total establishment was 400 all ranks, but this was rarely achieved. Rifle Troops consisted of 65 all ranks, each Section being 30 strong divided into 10 strong Sub-Sections. The average Heavy Weapons Troop consisted of all ranks manning 3-in mortars and Vickers machine guns.

recapture Termoli, forcing most of 11 Bde to withdraw. Heavy rain then washed away the RE's Bailey bridge over the River Bifurno, cutting the town off from the south and isolating the defenders. The battle continued for the next three days but on 6 October, 38(Irish)Bde relieved Termoli, after which both Commandos returned to Bari.

In October, 2 SS Bde was formed in Italy with No 2, 9, 40, the recently-raised 43(RM)Cdo and supplemented by Belgian and Polish Troops No 10(Inter-Allied)Cdo. Over the next eight weeks, the formation gained operational experience around Monte Cassino and the River Garigliano.

Anzio

The Anzio landings were designed to divert German forces defending the Cassino sector. On 22 January

1944, No 9 and 43(RM)Cdos successfully established the beachhead on the Alban Hills and were replaced by 3 US Rangers before returning to Naples. Both Commandos returned to the Cassino sector, 43(RM)Cdo seizing three hills in opposed night attacks. On 2 March 40(RM)Cdo was despatched to Anzio and for the next twenty-six days helped to defend the precarious beachhead in a war of attrition against the LXXVI Pz Corps on a muddy and went landscape that resembled a First World War battlefield.

The Dalmatian Islands

By early 1944, Marshal Tito's communist Partisans were scattered along the Dalmatian coast. The Allies were persuaded to assist Tito and by May 40 and

43(RM)Cdo joined No 2 Cdo, who had landed in January on Vis island. Raiding the islands and mainland forced the Germans to withdraw their island garrisons, except from Brac. In late May, German airborne forces very nearly captured Tito and he asked for a division so that the Partisans could reorganise.

A 6000-strong force of British and Partisans under command of HQ 2 SS Bde landed on Brac on 2 June. The two Royal Marine Commandos were tasked to night assault Hill 622, which overlooked the objective, a heavily defended four-gun battery. Unfortunately a signals breakdown and the Partisan refusal to attack meant the assault was made with the Commandos attacking in succession, which allowed the German defenders to deal with them piecemeal. The Force Commander, the charismatic bagpipe blowing Col. Jack Churchill, was captured and the mortally wounded Lt.Col. 'Pop' Manners, CO 40(RM)Cdo, died after being taken prisoner. On 4 June, the Brigade withdrew off Brac. The raiding policy continued and was often supported by the Raiding Support Regiment (RSR) close artillery, anti-tank and air defence support from such vessels as the LC (Gun). In late September 40(RM)Cdo spent some weeks in Albania and then on 9 October joined No 2 Cdo to capture Corfu, where it remained before going to Greece to intercede in the ferocious civil war. In mid-October, 43(RM)Cdo were withdrawn to Italy, but on 20 October landed at Dubrovnik and harried the German XXI Mountain Corps retreat through Yugoslavia. One Troop was converted into muleteers for another Troop which crewed 75mm mountain guns, but relations with the Partisans deteriorated further and on 20 January 1945, the Commando left the islands.

Lake Comacchio

The reassembled 2 Cdo Bde was ordered to seize Lake Comacchio, near Ravenna, on the 8th Army right flank and considered to be key to the German left flank. The defenders were mainly former prisoners from Soviet Asia Minor and a 42 Jaeger Div battalion. The ground was featureless and flooded and parts of the lake very shallow. On 2 April the Brigade attacked. Nos 2 and 9 Cdos crossed the lake and secured the north bank of the River Reno, supported by a 40(RM)Cdo feint. 43(RM)Cdo advanced north and linked up with No 2 Cdo by evening. Casualties were heavy. The advance continued the following day, during which Cpl. Tom Hunter of 43(RM)Cdo was awarded posthumously the only Royal Marine Victoria Cross of the Second World War, for attacking several enemy positions with his Bren gun. By 3 April 2 Cdo Bde had secured the right flank for 8th Army and was relieved the following night.

The Brigade returned to the line on 10 April when 40(RM)Cdo crossed the lake and attacked Marete Bridge on the western shore, which allowed V Corps to break out of the Argenta defile. The bridge was badly damaged and toggle ropes were used to fashion one. On 20 April 2 Cdo Bde was withdrawn from the line and three weeks later the war in Europe ended.

North West Europe

Normandy

Arguably 6 June 1944 was the most significant day in the history of Combined Operations with about 17,000 Royal Marines taking part in the landings and subsequent operations. The crossing was unpleasant with the landing craft being tossed around on choppy seas, but on a dull morning, the first assault infantry divisions began the run-in to the beaches.

1 SS Bde was tasked with linking up with 6th Airborne Division (6 AB Div) to form the eastern flank protection of the beachhead along the River Orne. Unique to this Brigade was that every Commando had a parachute-trained Troop and thus two members of E Tp 45(RM)Cdo dropped with 9 Para with whom 45(RM)Cdo expected to link up. Accompanying its associated three Army Commandos, 45(RM)Cdo landed on the left flank of SWORD (British) Beach about H+2 and pushing inland, linked up with the airborne forces holding the bridges across the River Orne advancing into the area around Franceville Plage.

4 SS Bde was tasked with securing the right and left flanks of SWORD and JUNO (Canadian) beaches respectively before moving inland to clear German positions. 41(RM)Cdo came ashore with 3(British)Div on SWORD Beach under heavy fire

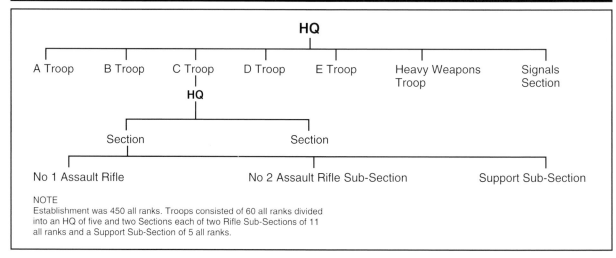

Royal Marine Commando – North West Europe (1944)

```
                              HQ
  ┌──────┬──────┬──────┼──────┬─────────────┬──────────┐
A Troop B Troop C Troop D Troop E Troop  Heavy Weapons  Signals
                HQ                         Troop        Section
          ┌─────┴─────┐
       Section      Section
   ┌──────────┬──────────────────────┬────────────────────┐
No 1 Assault Rifle   No 2 Assault Rifle Sub-Section    Support Sub-Section
```

NOTE
Establishment was 450 all ranks. Troops consisted of 60 all ranks divided into an HQ of five and two Sections each of two Rifle Sub-Sections of 11 all ranks and a Support Sub-Section of 5 all ranks.

Left: 40 Cdo RM patrol in Borneo, 1962. (RM Museum)

Wessex helicopter lands marines in a jungle clearing in Borneo, 1966. (RM Museum)

about 200 yards west of the landing point and, having crossed the beach and divided into Force 1 and 2, made for their objectives at Lion-sur-Mer. An unsuccessful assault on the second one cost the life of the CO, Lt.Col. Tim Gray; it was captured with 5 South Lancashires the following day. 46(RM)Cdo remained a floating reserve. With RMASG in support, 47(RM)Cdo landed in some confusion under fire on GOLD (British) and spent the whole day fighting to reach Port en Bassin, which was between GOLD and OMAHA (US) beaches. As 48(RM)Cdo approached JUNO Beach behind 3(Canadian)Div at St Aubin, some of its LCI (Small) became entangled in beach defences. Although the Canadians were pinned down under intense fire, Heavy Weapons Tp, still on board their landing craft, hastily arranged a 2-mortar smoke screen but even so the Royal Marines immediately suffered casualties as they clambered down the heaving ramps. To add to the chaos of the Commando becoming mixed up with Canadians, a LST disgorged Sherman tanks amongst the confusion on the surf line. Eventually the CO, Lt.Col. Jim Moulton, led his battered Commando off JUNO to clear houses overlooking the beaches but failing to contact 41(RM)Cdo, as planned, 48(RM)Cdo withdrew to Langrune.

The Allies consolidated the beachhead and both brigades held their sectors in bitter fighting in the bocage as the Germans attempted to breach the perimeter. 46(RM)Cdo and the Canadian Regiment de Chaudiere fought one of the roughest battles of the beachhead battle when they clashed with 12 SS Hitler Jugend Div in Le Hamel village. On 12 June, both SS brigades moved into the Seine line and for six weeks held important features against determined opposition. Life was rigorous; the mosquitos were most annoying and the month in foxholes on 'compo' rations and under constant threat of the enemy sapped their fighting edge. During the 18 July Operation GOODWOOD, both brigades were flank protection for the armoured thrust. On 1 August, during the Operation COBRA breakout, 1 SS Bde infiltrated enemy positions while 4 SS Bde advanced through thick woods and streams and captured Dozule. 1 SS Bde was halted at Beuzeville and remained there until 7 September. 4 SS Bde crossed the Seine on 31 August and then spent a month containing the German garrison at Dunkirk. Both were then withdrawn, 1st, with 45(RM)Cdo transferred, to UK having lost 50 per cent of its strength. 4 SS Bde, including No 4 Cdo which replaced the depleted 46(RM)Cdo, trained for the projected assault on Walcheren.

Walcheren

On 4 September, the British 11 Armd Div captured Antwerp and provided the Allies with a valuable deep water harbour but the approaches were occupied by the German Army, who by 1944 had converted the island into a formidable fortress with several batteries. The task of clearing these obstacles fell to the Dieppe veteran 2(Canadian) and 52(Lowland)Divs and 4 SS Bde, whose objective was Walcheren. A high dyke kept out the sea although this was breached at Westkapelle by Bomber Command Lancasters on 3 October. The plan called for No 4 Cdo to capture Flushing while the three Royal Marine Commandos landed on three beaches astride the breach and then break out left and right to roll up the defences. Early on 1 November No 4 and Norwegian and Dutch Tps, 10(Inter-Allied)Cdos landed at Flushing and moved into the town. To the north, 41(RM)Cdo successfully landed across RED Beach against severe opposition and swung north. On WHITE Beach, although its Heavy Weapons Tp lost most of the Vickers machine guns when its Buffalos were sunk, 48(RM)Cdo came ashore and turned south. Summoning air, artillery and naval gunfire support, the Commando neutralised a defiant battery causing chaos on the offshore gunline and amongst the landing craft approaching the beaches. 47(RM)Cdo landed in some confusion on GREEN Beach astride the breach, reorganised and also advanced south. The following day, it became involved

Sgt. J. Ellis of 40 Cdo RM on exercise Enchanter in Malaysia, January 1969.

Note the AR-15 rifle. (RM Museum)

in some heavy street fighting in Flushing, but linked up with No 4 Cdo and spent the next few days mopping up enemy resistance. 4 SS Bde lost about 40 per cent of its strength in the eight days of fighting.

On 6 December the SS Gp was renamed the Commando Group and the SS Bdes were retitled Commando Brigades. There was much relief throughout that any association with the German SS, even the initials, could now be ignored.

Advance into Germany

Although still weak, 4th Commando Brigade (4 Cdo Bde) returned to Walcheren in early December and was placed under command of 1(Canadian)Corps. Shortly after Christmas, it moved to the River Maas sector where it operated for the remainder of the war, tying down German troops. In late December, 1 Cdo Bde, which had expected to go to the Far East and now included 45 and 46(RM)Cdos, returned to Europe during the German Ardennes offensive and also took up positions along the River Maas. All the Commandos were involved in several patrol actions and raids in bitterly cold weather. Assigned then for the advance through Holland, 1 Cdo Bde came under command 7 Armd Div. During operations on 23 January 1945 to clear the Roermond area, 45(RM)Cdo captured Montefortebeck, during which LCpl Eric Harden RAMC was posthumously awarded the VC for tending wounded under fire.

The Rhine Crossings

On 23 March, 1 Cdo Bde spearheaded the Rhine crossing with 46(RM)Cdo crossing in Buffalos against opposition stunned by heavy air raids, followed by No 6 Cdo in stormboats coxswained by RM Engr Cdo sappers. 45(RM)Cdo then crossed and by nightfall the town of Wesel had been entered. The following day, contact was made with XVIII(US)AB Corps east of the town, which finally fell on 25 March after some stiff street fighting. 1 Cdo Bde joined the advance into Germany and after crossing several more rivers and canals stood on the shores of the Baltic by 8 May. Enemy units engaged included 12 SS Training Bn on the Weser and the German 2 Marine Div and a SS training battalion on the Aller.

1: Marine, Faroe Islands, April 1940
2: Oerlikon Gunner, RM Landing Craft, D-Day, 6 June 1944
3: Marine Gun Number, 'X' Turret, HMS Duke of York, December 1943

A

1: RM Fighter Pilot, Battle of Britain 1940
2: Marine, 41 (RM) Commando, Sicily, July 1943
3: Cpl., 'A' Commando, Dieppe 1942

B

1: Cyclist, 'A' Troop, 45 (RM) Commando, 1944
2: K Gun Ammunition Carrier, 'E' Troop, 45 (RM) Commando, Normandy 1944
3: L/Cpl., 'A' Troop, 47 (RM) Commando, Port-en-Bessin, Normandy 1944

C

1: Centaur Crewman, 5th Independent Battery, RM Armoured Support Group, Normandy 1944
2: Lt. Col., 48 (RM) Commando, 1944
3: Radio Operator, 'X' Troop, 33 RM Section, 30 Assault Unit, 1945

D

1: Sergeant, 44 (RM) Commando, Arakan Beachead, January 1945
2: Marine, 41 (Independent) Commando, Korea 1950
3: Royal Marine, 45 Commando, Suez 1956

E

1: Lt. Col., 42 Commando, July 1958
2: Commandant General, Royal Marines, 1961
3: Commanding Officer, 42 Commando

F

1: Sergeant J. Ellis, 40 Commando, Malaysia 1969
2: Sergeant, 42 Commando, 1960
3: Marine, 45 Commando, The Radfan 1966

G

1: Marine, 45 Commando, Northern Ireland 1970
2: Marine, 41 Commando, 1975
3: Royal Marine Helicopter Crewman, 1979

H

1: Marine, 40 Commando, May 1982
2: Marine, 42 Commando, June 1982

1: Marine, Recce Troop, 41 Commando, 1980
2: Marine, 'M' Company, 42 Commando, Ulster, 1987
3: Marine, 'X' Company, 45 Commando, 1991

J

1: OR's beret badge, Kings Crown version
2: Officers beret badge, ERII version
3: Second World War issue parachute wings
4: Embroidered 'Royal Marine' flash with curved
   Second World War 'Commando' title and unit numbers

5: RM Seige Regiment, grenade sleeve badge, Second World War
6: Woven 'Cash tape' title with separate numbers, Second World War
7: 34th Amphibious Support Regiment embroidered flash
8: Royal Marine Engineers printed flash, Second World War
9: 117 Royal Marine Brigade embroidered flash, 1945

K

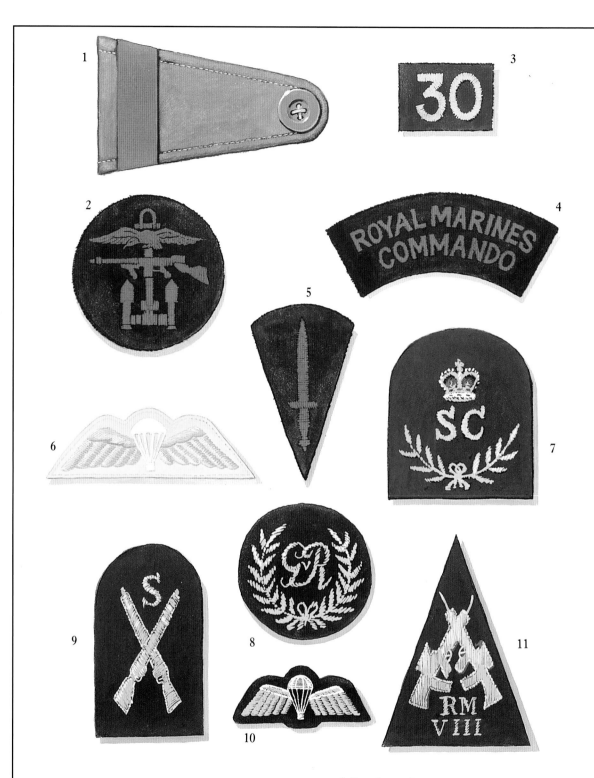

1: Coloured shoulder strap loop, 45 (RM) Commando, 1944
2: Combined operations flash, Second World War
3: 30 Assault Unit flash, Second World War
4: Embroidered 'Royal Marine Commando', 1946 to present day
5: Embroidered or printed dagger flash

6: Parachute wing tropical uniform
7: Swimmer canoeist 1, Lovat Suit
8: Kings Badge No. 1 and Lovat Suit
9: Royal Marine Sniper, Lovat Suit
10: Parachute wing No.1 Dress
11: Commandant General's shooting badge 1990, Lovat Suit

L

The Far East

On 6 November 1943 3 SS Bde was formed in the UK specifically for the Far East, consisting of the experienced No 1 and 5 Cdos and the recently raised 42 and 44(RM)Cdos. The formation arrived in Bombay in January 1944 minus No 1 and 42(RM)Cdos, who were in Egypt awaiting repairs to their ship which had been damaged in transit through the Mediterranean, and would subsequently arrive in September.

Arakan

3 SS Bde were welcome reinforcements to a theatre under intense threat from the Japanese and quickly committed to support 14th Army operations around Imphal and Kohima by raiding the west coast of Burma to keep Japanese forces off balance. In March both Commandos moved to Silchar to support 4 Corps' block to prevent the Japanese breaking into the Bengal Plain; 45(RM)Cdo had elephants on strength. The Brigade then moved to Ceylon where they were joined by No 1 and 42(RM)Cdos and began jungle training near Goa. In November the Brigade again raided the Arakan coastal plain. In December 1944, 3 SS Bde was named 3 Cdo Bde and today is the only survivor of the wartime SS formations. It carried out several operations, including the seizure of the Myebon peninsula in support of 15 Corps in January 1945. The Brigade was next ordered by 33 Corps to cut the Japanese 54 Inf Div's line of communications at Kangaw.

Kangaw

On 22 January 1945, 3 Cdo Bde set off up the Daingbong chaung in a long convoy of landing craft and landed in front of Hill 170, about two miles from Kangaw. No 1 Cdo seized the summit while 42(RM)Cdo moved onto 'Wilfred' and 44(RM)Cdo onto 'Pinner', which were two features to its east. Over the next ten days, 3 Cdo Bde battled with the Japanese Matsu Detachment determined to keep their lines of communication open. For some reason the Royal Marines would not use abandoned Japanese positions in spite of their robustness and were confined to their flooded shallow trenches. When 44(RM)Cdo withdrew to Daingbong village, having lost sixty casualties, 42(RM)Cdo moved onto Hill 170 and soon became involved in the intense fighting. On 31 January, they failed to recapture positions lost by No 1 Cdo. The fighting raged at short range with the Japanese swarming up the hill, frantically digging-in and then swarming up again, gradually inching their way up Hill 170 only to be shot down. Bren gun positions were vital; at one position 12 gunners were shot down in rapid succession. Two from three 19 Indian Lancers Shermans were damaged by Japanese suicide engineers and Lt. George Knowland (Royal Norfolks), of No 1 Cdo, was awarded a posthumous VC for several incidents of great courage when his Troop withdrew. During the night of 2 February, Matsu Detachment withdrew having lost over 400 against 120 casualties in 3 Cdo Bde during ten days of very heavy fighting.

3 Cdo Bde were withdrawn from Arakan and were trained for the invasion of Malaya, codenamed Operation 'Zipper', when the war in the Far East ended. It was then sent to Hong Kong to help supervise the liberation.

WO2 Rules and Cpl. Ratcliffe of 40 Cdo RM man an OP in the Episkopi Sovereign Base Area, Cyprus, 26 July 1974. (RM Museum)

POST-WAR OPERATIONS

The Army Commandos were disbanded by 1946 but the Royal Marines retained the Commando role and the green beret with 3rd Commando Brigade Royal Marines (3 Cdo Bde). 40(RM)Cdo was disbanded but resurfaced when 44(RM)Cdo was renumbered 40 Commando Royal Marines (40 Cdo). 42 and 45 Cdos also survived. In 1947, Plymouth became the centre for commando and amphibious training as National Servicemen were drafted in, most of the 9000 serving with 3 Cdo Bde over the next twenty-two years. All entrants were trained initially at the Royal Marines Depot in Deal and then moved to the Infantry Training Centre at Lympstone, now the Commando Training Centre Royal Marines, where the coveted green beret is earned. In 1948, the Royal Marine Volunteer Reserve (RMVR), now the Royal Marine Reserve (RMR), was formed, many of whom served as reinforcements in operational theatres.

Palestine

By 1946 3 Cdo Bde was in Malta when orders were received for its three Commandos to support the end of the British Mandate. Under command of 1 Guards Bde in Haifa, they were subjected to sniping, stoning, ambushes and riots inspired by the Jewish terrorists. 40 Cdo was the last British unit to quit Palestine on 27 June 1947, leaving the turmoil in the new Israel to burst into open warfare with the Arabs. Some Royal Marines then guarded Jewish displaced people in Cyprus.

In 1949, 3 Cdo Bde returned to Hong Kong to garrison duty dispersed with patrolling the border with the volatile People's Republic of China (PRC). In May 1950, it moved to Malaya to fight the Malayan Communist Party (MCP) insurgents engaged in its independence campaign.

Malaya

Perak is about the size of Wales with flat plains and rain-soaked jungle mountains. 40 Cdo was based around Kuala Kangsar, 42 Cdo near Ipoh and 45 Cdo at Tapah. Although 42 Cdo had been involved in the Burma campaign, jungle warfare training seems to have been lacking, but the patrols soon became competent against the highly experienced guerillas, most of whom were British-trained and equipped to fight the Japanese. Iban trackers were often used to trail guerilla spoors. Patrols were often fruitless but ambushes were set and Communist Terrorist (CT) camps attacked but by the end of the two years, the Brigade had accounted for 221 CTs at the expense of 30 Royal Marines. Lt. Jeremy Moore won the first of his two Military Crosses during an ambush.

3 Cdo Bde was then drafted to Malta as part of the Middle East Strategic Reserve, the Commandos being committed on rotation to Egypt on Canal Zone internal security duties.

Korea

On 25 June 1950, in an attempt to unify Korea, Communist North Korean forces crossed the 38th Parallel into South Korea and drove the ill-prepared South Korean and United Nations (UN) forces into

Mne Steve Freddi of 41 Cdo RM and a Danish member of UNFICYP, *Cyprus January 1975. (RM Museum)*

Royal Marines on riot control duties during a 'Battle of the Boyne'
march, c. 1970. (RM Museum)

headlong retreat to Pusan. The first Royal Marines to deploy were ten volunteers from the Far East Fleet's ships' detachments. In response to a demand for more raiding forces in Korea, 41 Cdo was resurrected as 41(Independent)Commando (41(Indep)Cdo). 219 volunteers assembled at Bickleigh when it was decided that the unit should fly to Japan incognito. Unfortunately few of the volunteers possessed civilian clothes and the Admiralty had to buy suits. Collecting more men from 3 Cdo Bde in Malaya, the Commando arrived in Japan on 15 September where they were issued United States Marine Corps (USMC) clothing and equipped with American weapons. However, they were to retain the green beret and British rank insignia; most also retained their trusted boots and sturdy battledress. On 2 October the Commando embarked in two US destroyers and carried out several raids against railways, tunnels and bridges along the North Korean eastern coast.

Meanwhile, the UN had advanced well into North Korea and 41(Indep)Cdo was ordered to join 1(US)Mne Div, who were strung out along the Hungham to Chosin road. On 10 November, 41(Indep)Cdo set off and encountered not only UN forces in full retreat but also the Chinese who had entered the war that day and had isolated several 1(US)Mne Div units. Burma veteran Lt.Col. Drysdale was ordered to relieve HQ 1(US)Mne Div, who were isolated at Hagaru-ri, 11 miles north along

Marine of L Company, 42 Cdo RM on patrol in
Belfast, c. 1976. (RM Museum)

a narrow valley road, aptly named 'Hellfire Valley'. In bitterly cold weather, the 900-strong mixed Royal Marines and USMC Task Force 'Drysdale' fought off sustained mass attacks and reached Hagaru-ri, losing over 300 men, 61 Royal Marines declared missing. 41(Indep)Cdo helped to defend the precarious perimeter and became known as the 'Chosin Few'. On 6 December, 1(US)Mne Div retreated down 'Hellfire Valley' to the coast, during which 41(Indep)Cdo joined 5(US)Mne as the rearguard and although cut off for a short time, it and 1(US)Mne Div reached the 10(US)Corps perimeter at Majong-Dong as did several Royal Marines who had been cut off in November. For their involvement in this epic battle, 41(Indep)Cdo were awarded a US Presidential Unit Citation. The Commando was then rested in Japan, where reinforcements brought it up to strength.

In April 1951, coming under command of the Commonwealth Division, 41(Indep)Cdo again raided the North Korean coast and then with South Korean Marines occupied several islands behind enemy lines. From these islands, they harassed the North Korean coast using canoes and landing craft to attack batteries and ambush patrols, forcing the Communist forces to reinforce the coastal defences. In December, 41(Indep)Cdo returned to England and was disbanded on 22 February 1952. 31 Royal Marines were killed in Korea and 17 survived harsh captivity, although one refused repatriation.

The Cyprus Emergency

In April 1955, the Greek–Cypriot EOKA revolt broke out in Cyprus and 3 Cdo Bde arrived from

Malta on 10 September as reinforcements. 40 Cdo deployed in Limassol and 45 Cdo patrolled the Kyrenia Range and within three months helped force EOKA to transfer its operating base to the Troodos Range. Both units worked closely with the police as they had done in Malaya. With the onset of winter, 45 Cdo joined the Gordon Highlanders in the Troodos Mountains to hinder EOKA guerilla operations in the rugged countryside. Dog techniques were developed with the Royal Army Veterinary Corps and X/45 Cdo were converted into ski troops by a Royal Horse Guards officer, so beginning a long association with winter warfare. In June, 45 Cdo took part in the operation to flush EOKA from the Troodos, during which a major forest fire claimed 19 Army lives but EOKA leader Col. George Grivas breached the cordon and reached Limassol. Meanwhile trouble was brewing in Egypt and in mid-summer 1956 3 Cdo Bde returned to Malta and began amphibious training.

40 and 45 Cdo returned to Cyprus to a campaign being fought with little evidence of success. The severe 1957 winter did give the Royal Marines the opportunity to develop their skiing skills and 45 Cdo developed helicopter techniques and created 45 HELFORCE with 728 NAS Whirlwinds, but not without incident. In one operation in the Panhandle, a heliborne 'stick' on a cordon and search was dropped in the wrong place and accidentally shot dead two Royal Marines already on the ground. In 1959, Cyprus was given its independence. The Royal Marines lost 10 killed during the EOKA campaign.

The Suez Campaign

In July 1956, Egyptian President Nasser nationalised the Suez Canal. The international response was for a military assault to repossess the Canal and 3 Cdo Bde, including 42 Cdo which was in the UK, was placed on stand-by for Op Musketeer. The brutal Soviet suppression of the Hungarian Uprising, the perceived collusion between the British, French and the Israelis to launch a pre-emptive ground offensive across the Sinai desert and the unpopularity of the venture caused political uncertainties about the wisdom of the operation. However, on 6 November, French and British amphibious and airborne troops landed near Port Said. 40 and 42 Cdos, supported by 6 Royal Tank Regiment Centurions, landed against

no opposition near the Suez Canal entrance and were clear of the beaches within 15 minutes. 40 Cdo seized the Port Said Suez Canal Company offices. 42 Cdo captured the Nile Cold Storage Company and the Power Station against considerable opposition from the Egyptian Army and police. 45 Cdo carried out the first vertical heliborne troop assault and landed in four waves on the Western breakwater, which signalled a close relationship between the Royal Marines and Fleet Air Arm (FAA) support helicopter units. It took the remainder of the day of confused street-fighting before 45 Cdo broke clear of the streets and linked up with 3 Para at Gamil Airport. By the end of the day, 3 Cdo Bde was firm covering a three-mile defensive zone. Nine Royal Marines had been killed and a further 60 wounded, which was about half of the total losses of the Anglo-French forces. Within the week, the Brigade less 42 Cdo had returned to Malta. 42 Cdo remained as part of 19 Inf Bde until relieved by UN Norwegian troops, after which it returned to the UK.

One of the lessons learnt from the Suez campaign was the value of amphibious forces which resulted in a significant evolution in Royal Marine history. In 1960, HMS *Bulwark* was the first of three aircraft-carriers to be converted into a Landing Plat-

Royal Marine Commando – Suez (1956)

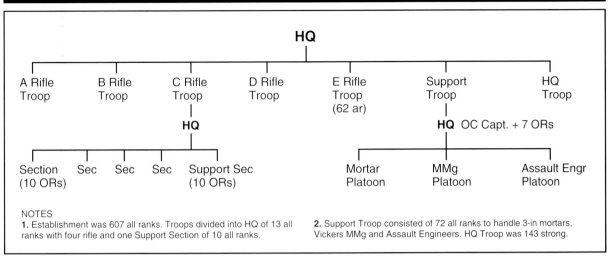

```
                                    HQ
        ┌──────┬──────┬──────┬──────┼──────┬──────────┬──────────┐
   A Rifle  B Rifle  C Rifle  D Rifle  E Rifle   Support      HQ
   Troop    Troop    Troop    Troop    Troop     Troop        Troop
                        │              (62 ar)      │
                       HQ                          HQ  OC Capt. + 7 ORs
   ┌──────┬────┬────┬────┬──────────┐        ┌──────────┬──────────────┐
 Section  Sec  Sec  Sec  Support Sec      Mortar      MMg        Assault Engr
 (10 ORs)                (10 ORs)         Platoon    Platoon       Platoon
```

NOTES

1. Establishment was 607 all ranks. Troops divided into HQ of 13 all ranks with four rifle and one Support Section of 10 all ranks.

2. Support Troop consisted of 72 all ranks to handle 3-in mortars, Vickers MMg and Assault Engineers. HQ Troop was 143 strong.

form Helicopter (LPH) commando carrier capable of lifting an expanded and self-supporting commando. Plans for a Commando to be permanently embarked on a commando carrier for strategic deployment and that any operations would be managed at unit level proved difficult as events in the Middle and Far East unfolded. The Royal Marines also had great difficulty persuading the Admiralty that a firm base for HQ 3 Cdo Bde was still needed, but eventually

Singapore was designated as the Fleet Amphibious Base Far East. 42 Cdo arrived in Singapore and remained for the next eleven years, dispersed with out of area operations. 40 Cde remained in Malta and 45 Cdo was drafted to Aden. 41 Cdo was reformed in 1960 and 43 Cdo in 1961. Plans to resurrect a UK based 4 Cdo Bde with these two units were shelved and they remained as strategic reserves. The term 'Company' replaced 'Troop' which was relegated to

Left: Marine of 45 Cdo on a Shell/Esso gas platform in the North Sea during an anti-terrorist exercise in 1975. (RM Museum)

Royal Marines mountain training in the Cairngorms in February 1962. (RM Museum)

identify Army platoon-sized units. The operational command structure through HQ Cdo Forces was located to Plymouth, first to Stonehouse Barracks and then to Hamoaze House, where it is today. In 1962 Army commandos reappeared with 29 Regt RA converted into Commando artillery and 40 Cdo arrived in Singapore. In 1963 95 Regt RA was converted a year later and 40(Dieppe), and 42(Kangaw)Air Tps were formed to support the Commando Recce Troops, as was 29(Brunei)Air Tp to provide air observation for 29 Cdo Light Regt RA.

The Defence of Kuwait

Midst the changes that 3 Cdo Bde were undergoing, the international scene remained unpredictable. In June 1961, Kuwait sought assistance from Great Britain to deter a threatened Iraqi invasion. The HMS *Bulwark* Amphibious Warfare Squadron was training in the Persian Gulf and on 1 July 42 Cdo was helicoptered to Mutla Pass to cover the Baghdad road and was then joined by 45 Cdo from Aden. Within the week the brigade group was reinforced by Army units. Both units remained ashore for three weeks, the intense heat severely straining the logistics, particularly the supply of fresh water. The operation was a success and the threat was deterred.

Mutiny in Tanganyika

In January 1962, four days after the 1st Tanganyika Rifles mutinied, President Nyerere sought help from Great Britain. 45 Cdo embarked on the carrier HMS *Centaur* and at dawn 25 January, were dropped near the Army barracks in Dar-Es-Salaam and Tabora and by 27 January had suppressed the mutiny.

Aden

During its time under British influence, Aden was divided into the urban Colony of about seventy square miles and the hinterland of the protectorate, which covers an area about the size of England. In 1962 Egypt encouraged regional anti-British propaganda and the Federation of Arab Emirates, which included Aden, sought protection from Great Britain. In December 1963, Aden degenerated into tribal and political feuding with rioting, grenade attacks and sniping on the local Security Forces by the National Liberation Front (NLF), who were nicknamed the 'Cairo Grenadiers'. In the desolate Radfan, Egyptian-backed dissident tribesmen, who called themselves 'The Red Wolves', threatened the *Doub el Haj* or Sacred Road, an ancient caravan route which ran from Aden, past Dhala to Mecca.

Capt. Bill Peart RM leads K Company, 42 Cdo RM on exercise in Norway, February 1986. (RM Museum)

Royal Marine Commando – Aden and Far East (1964)

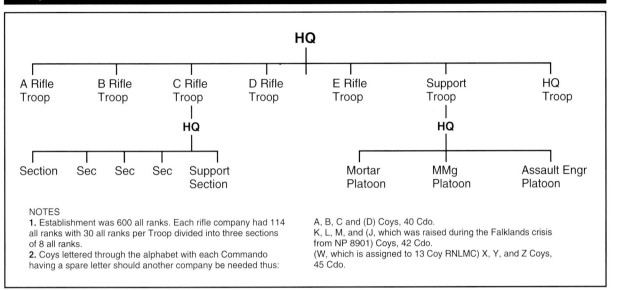

NOTES
1. Establishment was 600 all ranks. Each rifle company had 114 all ranks with 30 all ranks per Troop divided into three sections of 8 all ranks.
2. Coys lettered through the alphabet with each Commando having a spare letter should another company be needed thus:

A, B, C and (D) Coys, 40 Cdo.
K, L, M, and (J, which was raised during the Falklands crisis from NP 8901) Coys, 42 Cdo.
(W, which is assigned to 13 Coy RNLMC) X, Y, and Z Coys, 45 Cdo.

In January 1964, The Federal Regular Army (FRA) fought their way into the Radfan but when they withdrew, the tribesmen reoccupied the area. On 29 April, Radforce, which consisted of 45 Cdo, B/3 Para, A/22 SAS, J Battery 3 Royal Horse Artillery (J/3RHA) and combat and service support moved against the dissident tribesmen to demonstrate that nothing was safe, if they persisted in harassing the Sacred Road. The operation was full of hazards. The enemy knew the area well, were expert shots, courageous and were resentful of the British. The SAS patrol was ambushed, but the following day, 45 Cdo and 3 Para infiltrated deep into the Radfan and within six weeks dominated the area. Over the next two years the British reduced the tribesmen into small incohesive groups. A company group was always based at Dhala where, compared to the lowlands, life was cooler and thus the six-week tours bearable. The RAF could be relied to supply the mountain garrisons by helicopter and provide rapid fighter ground attack support with Hawker Hunters. Although the February 1966 Defence White Paper declared that Britain would leave Aden after South Arabia achieved independence, terrorism increased dramatically when the Front for the Liberation of South Yemen (FLOSY) began to rival the NLF. In June 1967, 45 Cdo handed over its Radfan bases to the South Arab Army and returned to Aden, where on 11 October they were reinforced by the HMS *Albion*-borne jungle-green clad 42 Cdo, diverted from Far East operations. Midst a colony tense with frequent shooting and civil unrest, the British evacuated the garrison. On 28 November 1967, after seven years in Aden, 45 Cdo were flown back to Plymouth to begin winter warfare training. 42 Cdo re-embarked the following day and returned to Singapore.

Indonesia

In the early 1960s, Indonesia threatened the federated Malaysian states in Borneo and in December 1962 inspired rebels in Brunei to occupy the capital and take hostages to Limbang in Sarawak, which was across the river. L/42 Cdo were deployed from Singapore and on 10 December, sailed up the river in two Royal Navy crewed ancient Z Lighters, attacked Limbang police station, killed several rebels and released the hostages for the loss of five Royal Marines and eight wounded in a vicious action that included an opposed landing. Capt. Jeremy Moore, who commanded the operation, was awarded his second MC. Nevertheless confrontation with Indonesia developed. HQ 3 Cdo Bde landed in Kuching in December 1962 and over the next four years intermittently returned to Borneo from Malaysia to conduct operations. This was a campaign conducted not only in the jungle but also along the coast, waterways and rivers in assault boats, local longboats and SRN-5 hovercraft. Helicopters were also a feature of the campaign. Initially jungle warfare techniques were lacking and 40 and 42 Cdos both suffered non-battle casualties. Formal training was instituted, which included each man deciding by which method he should carry his equipment. The Royal Marines continue jungle warfare training on regular 'Curry Trails' in Brunei. With the assistance of Iban trackers and Border Scouts, Indonesian Army patrols were intercepted, ambushed and harried as they attempted to penetrate the states with the Commandos recording kills. SB Sections were also active. Confrontation finally ended in August 1966 when Indonesia recognised that Britain would continue to support the Malaysian federation.

In 1965, the familiar lovat green uniform was introduced to replace battledress and as alternative to 'blues'. Combat uniforms and equipment remained identical to that of the Army, although the Corps did sometimes allow the Royal Marines some latitude. The 7.62mm L1A1 Self Loading Rifle was introduced in 1967. Although commando carriers had proven their flexibility from over the horizon when least expected to tackle an emergency, the 1968 Defence White Paper had serious implications for the Corps, as indeed it had throughout the Armed Forces. With the complete withdrawal from the Far East, the Royal Marines strategic role was redefined to NATO's Allied Forces Northern Europe (AFNORTH) and specified Out of Area operations. The Corps' strength was reduced to about 8000 and 43 Cdo and 95 Cdo Light Regt RA were disbanded. The commando carriers were replaced by the Landing Platforms Dock (LPD). HMS *Fearless* and *Intrepid*. In August 1968, the 3 Commando Brigade Air Squadron (3 Cdo BAS) was formed in Singapore and specialist sapper support arrived when 59 Field Squadron RE was converted to 59 Independent Commando Engineer Squadron RE (59 Indep Cdo Sqn RE) in 1971.

NORTHERN IRELAND

Meanwhile, the security situation in Ulster had deteriorated to the point that the Army was called in to separate the two communities. In September 1969, 41 Cdo, then serving as 'Spearhead Battalion' of the Strategic Reserve, was deployed to Belfast, and began regular four-, and latterly six-month, roulement tours in the Province. In July 1972, 40 and 42 Cdos participated in Operation 'Motorman' to demolish the Republican and Loyalist No-go areas that had developed in Londonderry and Belfast, The same month, Marine Allen of 40 Cdo was the first Royal Marine to be killed when he was shot by a sniper in

Royal Marines receive Bren gun instruction during arctic trials on HMS Vanguard *in the winter of 1949. (RM Museum)*

Belfast. By then one hundred Army personnel had been killed in the line of duty.

At the time, 'Motorman' was the largest operation undertaken by the Army and Royal Marines since Suez. The mission for the commanding officers of the battalions and Commandos committed to 'Motorman' was to 'establish a continuing presence in all hard areas in order to dominate extremists and thus neutralise their ability to influence events until a political settlement has been achieved'.

Since 1972 over twenty years have passed with numerous attacks being perpetrated upon the security forces and not just aimed at the foot soldiers. In 1979 Lord Mountbatten, Life Commandant General, was killed while on holiday in Eire, and two years later Lt.Gen. Sir Stuart Pringle, Commandant General Royal Marines, lost a leg when his car was booby-trapped by an explosive device in London.

While Royal Marines are no longer faced by rioting crowds in Northern Ireland, they continue to undertake tours of duty in the Province. The particular tactical strengths of the Corps mean that they often serve along the border in the 'bandit territory' of South Armagh. Patrolling in areas which have considerable natural cover, as well as covert Observation Posts (OPs) is testing for even the fittest men, winters and autumns can be cold and damp and the IRA a wily and experienced enemy. The small-boat skills of the Royal Marines mean that they are expert at patrols along Carlingford Lough which marks the border between Northern Ireland and the Republic. The Royal Marines have received numerous decorations for service in Northern Ireland including a George Medal for gallantry.

THE FALKLANDS AND THE GULF

The Falklands Campaign

In mid-March 1982 a small band of Argentinian scrap metal merchants landed on South Georgia, which precipitated Great Britain and Argentina to war. Early on 2 April, the Argentinian Amph Cdo Coy landed near Stanley and forced the surrender of the tiny NP 8901. In UK, 3 Cdo Bde, commanded by Brig. Julian Thompson, was warned for deployment south, although some elements were still on their way back from Norway. By 17 April the Amphibious Task Force had assembled at Ascension Island, which became a rear logistic base. 40 Cdo carried out several sweeps of the island for suspected Argentinian Special Forces; none were found. On 25 April M/42 Cdo joined the Advanced Forces to recapture South Georgia. On 21 May, 3 Cdo Bde landed at San Carlos Water, which precipitated a hectic period as 3 Cdo Bde struggled ashore amidst heroic attempts by the Argentinian Air Force to disrupt the schedule. 3 Cdo BAS lost two Gazelles shot down by retreating

Royal Marine Commando – Falklands Campaign (1982)

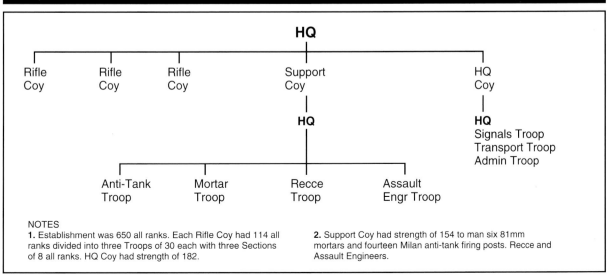

NOTES

1. Establishment was 650 all ranks. Each Rifle Coy had 114 all ranks divided into three Troops of 30 each with three Sections of 8 all ranks. HQ Coy had strength of 182.

2. Support Coy had strength of 154 to man six 81mm mortars and fourteen Milan anti-tank firing posts. Recce and Assault Engineers.

Argentinians. The beachhead was secured, although the Cdo Log Regt and 45 Cdo took casualties when the Ajax Bay refrigeration plant was bombed. On 28 May, 2 Para defeated the Goose Green garrison, during which its Commanding Officer, Lieut.Col. 'H' Jones, was posthumously awarded the Victoria Cross. 5 Inf Bde then arrived and Land Forces Falkland Islands (Maj.Gen. Jeremy Moore MC* RM) was formed. On 31 May, both Brigades broke out of the beachhead, with 5 Inf Bde taking the southerly route along the track to Fitzroy. 3 Cdo Bde took the rigorous northerly route and were helped when a Mountain and Arctic Warfare Cadre (M&AW Cadre) patrol attacked an Argentinian 602 Cdo Coy section at Top Malo House, 40 Cdo guarded the Brigade Maintenance Area (BMA), while the Cdo Log Regt wrestled with moving supplies and equipment. On 12 June, 3 Para overwhelmed elements of Argentinian 7 Inf Regt on Mt Longdon, during which Sgt. Mick McKay was posthumously awarded the Victoria Cross. 45 Cdo captured Two Sisters and 42 Cdo Mt Harriet from the 4 Inf Regt, the latter after a 1 Welsh Guards group, which included 40 Cdo, secured their Start Line. 5 Inf Bde then attacked 5 Mne Inf Bn on Mt Tumbledown and 2 Para, under command of 3 Cdo Bde, attacked the remainder of 7 Inf Regt on Wireless Ridge. The Argentinians surrendered on 14 June and a month later the majority of 3 Cdo Bde returned to Southampton on the SS *Canberra*.

Following the Falklands campaign, British strategic thinking re-examined the feasibility of despatching forces on Out of Area Operations. The Joint Force Headquarters (JFHQ) was formed to manage such operations with HQ 3 Cdo Bde and 5 AB Bde as principal components. Several command post and troop exercises practised the new role with, in 1986, 40 Cdo deploying to Oman on 'Saif Sareea' and trialled the new SA-80 5.56mm Rifle.

Above: Mne Williams of 40 Cdo RM lands at Namsos, Norway during the international exercise Teamwork, October 1990. (RM Museum)

579 Assault Squadron RM rigid raider with USMC passengers, exercise Dragon Hammer, Sardinia, May 1987. (RM Museum)

The Gulf War

Though 42 and 40 Cdo were in Norway and 45 Cdo in Northern Ireland during Operation Granby, the British forces deployment to the Gulf in 1990–91, there were individual Marines ashore in Saudi Arabia and NP 1028, 1029 and 1030 provided the boarding parties for HMS *London*, *Brazen*, *Gloucester* and *Cardiff* as well as air defence and upper deck sentries for the Royal Fleet Auxiliary supply ships. RFA *Argus* also carried many members of the Royal Marines Band Service working as stretcher bearers and first aid reception parties.

Air defence capability for the RFAs was provided by shoulder held javelin missiles manned by Royal Marines from Air Defence Troop, 3 Cdo Bde HQ and Sigs Sqn and soldiers of 21 Air Defence Bty 47 Fd Rgt RA.

Operation Safe Haven was a real challenge for the Corps. From the beginning, 3 Cdo Bde (minus 42 Cdo) worked as part of a multi-national force which at the height of the crisis was composed of 23,000 troops from 13 nations. The Kurdish refugees, some 500,000, had fled into the inhospitable mountains of northern Iraq, pressed back by murderous Iraqi army and Republican Guard forces. Between April and July the Royal Marines worked hard on the priorities of shelter, food, clean water and sanitation. The US Army and Marines watched with appreciation how professionally 45 Cdo, freshly returned from Northern Ireland, patrolled in 'multiples' through the disputed towns of northern Iraq. There were some brief fire fights with Iraqi Republican Guards, who scuttled away when they realised the calibre of the opposition. Not only was 3 Cdo Bde involved in humanitarian work, it also cleared many of the mines laid by the Iraqis in their brutal war against the Kurds as well as unexploded ordnance from Coalition air attacks.

The Future

The Royal Marines escaped the savage 1992 Options for Change and 1994 Front Line cuts and their future seems assured with a commitment to replace the two LPDs. The Corps is now part of the United Kingdom strategic response with 5 AB Bde and some Army formations. Its lack of mechanised experience has precluded a Commando serving with the UN Protection Force (UNPROFOR) in Bosnia although individuals served with 845 and 846 NAS during their deployments.

Bibliography

Beaver, Paul, *Today's Royal Marines* (1988), Thorsons Publishing Group.

Ladd, James, *Commandos and Ranger of World War Two*, Book Club Associates.

Ladd, James, *The Royal Marines* (1980), Jane's, London.

Messenger, Charles, *The Commandos* (1985), William Kimber & Co. Ltd, London.

Neillands, Robin, *By Sea and Land* (1987), George Weidenfeld & Nicholson Ltd, London.

'X' Troop of 40 Cdo RM hoisting the White Ensign at Navy House Port Said 1956. (W. Fowler)

THE PLATES

A1: Marine, Faroe Islands, April 1940

This marine from 'Force Sandall' landed from HMS *Suffolk* on 12th April 1940, and is virtually indistinguishable from his counterparts in the First World War. He wears 1902 service dress of the modified pattern first issued in the early 1920s. Note the soft 'Trench' cap with stitched peak still being worn at this date, and his blancoed 1908 pattern webbing equipment. The long puttees are being worn with the service dress trousers turned down to give a deep 'plus fours' effect. He is armed with an SMLE No 1 MkIII.

A2: RM Landing Craft, Oerlikon Gunner D-Day

An exhausted marine of LCG(L) 1007 takes some much needed sleep after the initial bombardment on D-Day, 6th June 1944. He wears a typical combination of warm naval kit used by these gun crews. Here the duffle coat with anti-flash hood and gloves worn underneath is worn over blue battledress tucked into heavy leather sea boots. Over this he wears the RN life preserver and grey painted steel helmet. A magazine for his 20mm Oerlikon gun lies at his side. Landing Craft Gun (Large) 1007a Mk4 vessel of 333

Support Flotilla, had been in action off Juno beach early on the morning of D-Day.

A3: Marine Gun Number, 'X' Turret, HMS Duke of York December 1943

During *Duke of York*'s pursuit of the *Scharnhorst*, this gun number wears a blue RN boiler suit under anti-flash gloves and hood. He has the RN pattern anti-gas respirator in its case (note the extra waist strap on these cases). The steel helmet is worn with it's chin strap at the back of the head. The life preserver was always worn when in action.

B1: Royal Marine Fighter Pilot, Battle of Britain 1940

One of 3 RM pilots attached to RAF Fighter Command during the Battle of Britain, Captain Alan Marsh wears khaki battledress under a 1932 pattern life jacket. He holds his Type B flying helmet with its MkIII goggles and Type D oxygen mask. His flying boots are of the 1936 pattern.

B2: Marine, 41 (RM) Commando, Sicily, July 1943

During an inspection prior to the Sicily landings this marine wears the 4 pocket KD bush jacket and '37 pattern webbing. Note the toggle rope secured around the shoulders, the assault life jacket and two

Royal Marines of 45 Cdo Group on exercise Cold Winter in Norway, March 1987. (RM Museum)

Right: CGRM Sir John Richards and Capt. S.J. Jones the CO of the Base Company, 45 Cdo Group RM, with the dog section at RM Condor, Arbroath, November 1979. (RM Museum)

50 round cotton bandoliers of .303 ammunition for his SMLE No 1 MkIII*. He wears short pattern puttees which were then coming into use. '41 RM' was amongst the first units to use the 'Battle Jerkin' in action and also the light pattern respirator.

B3: Royal Marine Corporal, 'A' Commando, Dieppe 1942

Depicted here on his return from the raid, this cpl. wears '37 pattern battledress and '37 pattern webbing equipment. Note the life preserver, toggle rope and knuckle duster knife attached to the waistbelt. He wears two straight, woven titles 'Royal Marines' with 'Commando' beneath, both in red on dark blue. He has a slung respirator and is armed with a Thompson sub-machine gun.

C1: Cyclist 'A' Troop 45 (RM) Commando, 1944

A marine of '45 RM' in the assembly area for the Normandy landings, 3 June 1944. He wears the 'Bren vest' over his '40 pattern battledress and a '37 pattern haversack on his back held by its 'L' straps. He does not at this stage wear his assault life jacket. The green beret was worn without cap badge by this unit. He still has an army pattern steel helmet strapped, along with the toggle rope, to a paint-streak camouflaged bergen rucksack. A strip of Vickers machine gun

ammo belt has been sewn to the upper part of the battledress trousers. This held several types of .303 round (tracer, ball, armour piercing), so that the firer could select a particular type of ammunition as required.

C2: K Gun Ammunition Carrier 'E' Troop 45 (RM) Commando, Normady 1944

The Vickers 'K' Gun was deployed in small numbers to provide additional firepower in forward positions because of its high rate of fire – a possible 950 to 1100 rpm. It was to prove impractical in use due to the amount of ammunition expanded and was discarded after the break out from Normandy. This marine has the webbing pouched provided for 'K' gun drum magazines. These attached to the braces and waistbelt of the '37 pattern set. He also carries a 50-round cotton bandolier of .303 cartridges for his SMLE No 4 rifle. Note the red shoulder strap loops worn by this unit, 41 and 48 RM cdo's also used coloured loops

C3: L/Cpl. 'A' Troop 47 (RM) Commando, Port-en-Bessin, Normandy 1944

This Cdo was the only one to be completely equipped with the 'Battle Jerkin' for the D-Day landings although this was unpopular and was replaced as quickly as circumstances would allow. Much of this units' kit was lost during the landings including most heavy weapons, only 'B' and 'X' troops landing intact. Much use was made of captured German weaponry and this L/Cpl. has armed himself with an MP40 sub-machine gun. He wears a knitted 'comforter' in place of a beret. 47 RM were not fully re-equipped for another month.

D1: Centaur Crewman, 5th Independent Battery, RM Armoured Support Group, Normandy 1944

This marine wears the blue beret with its red badge backing which replaced the khaki side cap during 1943. It was worn by all marines in combined operations from that year and by others not entitled to wear the green beret, which had been worn from late in 1942 by commando trained marines. This blue beret is still worn to the present day by all marines in training and until the successful completion of the commando course. (See MAA156 *Royal Marines*

1956–1984.) He wears khaki '37 pattern battledress trousers with what appears to be an RN blue pullover possibly acquired from 'slops', with issue trouser braces and a corps waistbelt.

D2: Lt.Col. 48 (RM) Commando, 1944

Commanding officer of 48 RM on D-Day, Lt.Col. James L. Moulton, who qualified as a pilot with the Fleet Air Arm in 1930, wears the 'faced' battledress adopted by officers with RN pilots wings above the left breast pocket. Below this is the ribbon of the 1939–1943 (as it was then known) which was first issued early in 1944. He wears his green beret with the 2-piece officers cap badge. '48 RM' landed on D-Day and captured an enemy strongpoint at Langrune-sur-Mer. During this attack the unit suffered 50% casualties. Lt.Col. Moulton was subsequently awarded the DSO.

D3: Radio Operator, 'X' Troop, 33 RM section, 30 Assault Unit, 1945

This marine operates a wireless set No 38 introduced in 1943 it had a range of four to five miles and was used for close communication. Note the throat microphone and the rod aerial case visible over his right shoulder. Powered by dry cell batteries, the whole set weighed 27lbs. The insignia of 30 Assault Unit is worn on both sleeves – straight 'Royal Marines' titles and a light blue '30' on a dark blue rectangle. Many marines in this unit had received parachute training and this marine wears his parachute wings between the unit insignia on the right arm. 30 Assault Unit was a mixed RN – RN unit specifically trained in intelligence gathering duties and at this time was tasked to secure the latest developments in German Naval technology.

Above: A Royal Marine in Norway uses his ski sticks to support a 7.62 mm L4A3 Light Machine Gun (LMG) fitted with a blank firing device during arctic warfare training. He wears a camouflaged waterproof nylon snow suit. (W. Fowler)

Swedish built Bandvangn Bv 202 over-snow vehicles in Norway. The Royal Marines took these to the Falklands in 1982 where they proved effective in negotiating the soft peat of the islands. They have now been replaced in the UK by the larger and more powerful Haaglund Bv 206. (W. Fowler)

E1: Sergeant 44 (RM) Commando, Arakan Beachead, January 1945

Armed with a Thompson sub-machine gun, this NCO wears the jungle green battledress top and trousers. He has an individually acquired American web pistol belt with a Colt .45 pistol in a US brown leather holster, a pair of binoculars and case, again possibly of US origin, a British flare pistol in its leather holster and a Bergen rucksack. He wears the short puttees introduced from 1943 and SV boots. He wear the ribbons of the Military Medal and the 1939–1943 star.

E2: Marine 41 (Independent) Commando, Korea 1950

41 (Independent) Commando was raised for the Korean War in August 1950. They were largely clothed and equipped by US forces but the green beret was still worn. This marine preparing explosive changes wears standard M1943 combat clothing with an OG wool shirt and white T-shirt underneath. He wears canvas shoes and woollen hose tops as gaiters. Note the British clasp knife hanging from the M1923 cartridge belt. He is armed with the US M1 Garand rifle. The beret is worn without cap badge in this instance.

E3: Royal Marine 45 Commando, Suez 1956

Marines of 45 Cdo carried out the first large scale helicopter assault during Operation Musketeer – the attack on Port Said. This Bren gunner is wearing an angola shirt, denim BD trousers, short puttees and SV boots. Note the Bren spares case slung around the body and the boot polish blackened '37 pattern webbing equipment. Anti-gas goggles were worn to provide protection from swirling sand.

F1: Lt.Col., 42 Commando, July 1958

This officer wears the 1949 pattern battledress then in use, with one piece 'Royal Marines Commando' title worn from 1946 to the present day. Below this is the dagger emblem worn by 3 Commando Brigade from just after World War Two until 1964. This badge is still used today by commando trained personnel other than Royal Marines. He has the dark blue RM officers lanyard on his left shoulder and the white lanyard of 42 Cdo on his right. Note the black boot polished webbing belt and gaiters – a practice in 3 Commando Brigade which dates from the late World War Two period. He wears SV boots.

F2: Commandant General, Royal Marines, 1961

General Sir Ian Riches is seen here wearing khaki tropical shirt and trousers with brown officers shoes. Note the bullion general officers badge on his beret and note that red gorget patches are unusually not worn in this instance on his shirt collar. A corps stable belt is worn.

F3: Commanding Officer, 42 Commando

Seen here after his promotion to colonel, but before he left 42 Cdo, CO P.J. Whitely wears olive green shirt and shorts. As a fixed wing pilot trained in the late 1940s he wears Royal Navy wings above the left breast pocket and he also wore a parachute qualifica-

A Royal Marine patrol led by a troop commander and headed by a dog handler during operations against EOKA terrorists on Cyprus. Dogs have been used in many post-war campaigns including Indonesia and Northern Ireland. These animals can be trained to detect weapons and explosives, as well as tracking men or guarding installations. (W. Fowler)

Men of the Reconnaissance Troop of 40 Cdo RM photographed soon after they were recovered from a deep patrol against the Indonesians in Borneo in the 1960's confrontation.

They wear drab jungle green uniforms, sweat rags, belt orders made from aircraft quick release straps, and are armed with the 5.56 mm M16 Armalite rifle. (W. Fowler)

tion wing on the upper right sleeve. Note the red gorget patches of his rank worn here and the dark blue officers lanyard on the left shoulder. He wears khaki hose tops with stone coloured officers puttees and the white garter tabs of 42 Cdo.

G1: Sergeant J. Ellis, 40 Commando, Malaysia 1969

Whilst taking part in Exercise Enchanter in Malaysia, January 1969, Sgt. Ellis wears jungle green shirt, trousers with side pocket, and bush hat. Note the black chevrons worn on the right sleeve only. He would have worn one of two patterns (long or short) of canvas jungle boot. The '58 pattern webbing is worn with carrier frame to which is strapped a '58 pattern large pack and sleeping bag rolled in a poncho. He is armed with an M16 rifle.

G2: Sergeant, 42 Commando, 1960

He wears a Denison smock over denim battledress trousers, short puttees and SV boots. The Denison smock was first issued to Royal Marines in the latter part of 1944 and was worn until the introduction of DPM camouflaged clothing in the early 1970s, however, they were often retained by individuals and still to be seen in the 1980s. He wears parachute wings on the upper right sleeve and the chevrons worn on the right sleeve only, have been whitened. The life jacket was worn for all landing exercises and helicopter trips over water. Note the company markings on the butt of his SLR. This rifle was first introduced in 3 Commando Brigade in 1959.

G3: Marine 45 Commando, The Radfan 1966

Royal Marines served in the Radfan from July 1964 to June 1967. The practical and comfortable rig adopted by this marine consists of KD shirt and rolled up KD shorts, KD bush hat, grey issue sock, puttees and SV boots. '58 pattern webbing is worn with 2 '44 pattern water bottle pouch. The plastic '58 pattern water bottle is retained however. He is draped with GPMG link.

H1: Marine 45 Commando, Northern Ireland, 1970

This marine wears clothing and equipment typical of early deployments to Ulster. He wears a US M69 body armour worn over the olive green combat jacket then on issue. He wears a belt order consisting of a '58 pattern belt with a single magazine pouch and on the right side a water bottle in its pouch. Note the SLR still at this time with wooden furniture and the sling looped around his right wrist to prevent the weapon being dropped or snatched. The beret badge has been blackened. Later body armour had British made covers attached.

H2: Marine, 41 Commando, 1975

Marine Steve Freddi a member of UNFICYP, Cyprus, January 1975 wears a woolly-pully with 'Royal Marine Command' titles, the blue beret with UN cap badge and UN sleeve badge. 'Lightweight' trousers are worn with short puttees and DMS boots which were first issued in the mid 1960s. Note the SLR now with black plastic furniture.

H3: Royal Marine Helicopter Crewman, 1979

This WO wears a standard green flying suit with a lightweight life jacket. Just visible is the 3 Commando Brigade Air Squadron badge on the upper right sleeve. His rank insignia are worn on slip-ons attached to the shoulder straps. An observers wing is worn on the upper left breast. Note the privately acquired (?) black leather gloves.

I1: Marine, 40 Commando, May 1982

This marine wears a rig typical for the early stages of Operation Corporate. '58 pattern equipment with several water bottle pouches replacing the 'kidney pouches'. Note his 'skid lid' hung by its chin strap from his left hand pouch. He wears 'lightweight' trousers used by some marines right through the campaign with heavy civilian walking boots and rolled hose tops. Note the 'headover' worn around his neck and the wristlet mittens being worn. He is armed with a 9 mm Sterling sub machine gun.

I2: Marine, 42 Commando, June 1982

Marine Steve Chubb, J Company, 42 Cdo is seen here in clothing and equipment used in the closing stages of the Falklands operation. Most marines wore newly issued kit in the South Atlantic particularly 'Juliet' company, a hastily raised company formed from the repatriated members of NP 8901 captured during the Argentine invasion. Marine Chubb was one of twenty three Marines under Lt. Keith Mills who were captured after their spirited defence of South Georgia in April 1982. Steve Chubb was to be very badly injured by shell splinters early on the 13th June 1982 after the capture of Mt Harriet by '42'. He wears the windproof smock and trousers with German para boots, which were privately acquired by some marines. He wears '58 pattern webbing without the 'bum roll' and with a respirator case added on the left-hand side which he used to carry GPMG link. The headover is again worn at the neck. He is armed with a SLR which he used without its sling attached.

Royal Marines of the Air Defence Tp armed with the Short Javelin low altitude surface-to-air missile system. The Marines wear trousers men's lightweight (TML's) wind-proof smocks, and '58' pattern webbing. The man on the right is armed with a 7.62 mm L1A1 self-loading rifle. (W. Fowler)

Also carried is a 66 mm LAW which saw widespread use against Argentine bunkers and positions during the campaign.

J1: Marine, Recce Troop, 41 Commando, 1980

Marine Brien Hobbs wears a typical patrol rig for wet weather, here a civilian Nevisport Orion jacket one of several acquired by this troop for their own use. Fighting order consists of two '58 magazine pouches and two water bottle pouches. Interestingly he wears privately acquired World War Two vintage 'Bren pouches' which have been camouflage painted. He wears the large 'airborne' or 'SAS' pattern bergen with a rolled sleeping mat under the flap. A total of 11 magazines for the 7.62 L4A4 LMG were carried, distributed in the vest and pouches. He wears tropical issue DPM trousers which were useful for their quick-drying qualities and the large pocket on each leg. He wears Patrick walking boots with khaki hose tops rolled over.

The particular requirements of patrolling in Northern Ireland and the poor quality and unsuitability of some of the kit issued during the 70s and 80s led to the widespread adoption of privately purchased items. This was actively encouraged at this time by most COs.

J2: Marine 'M' Company, 42 Commando, Ulster 1987

Marine Royston of 8 Troop, M company, 42 Cdo awaits a helicopter airlift to Crossmaglen in July 1987. Royal Marines were by this time almost indistinguishable from their Army counterparts. He wears the MK6 ballistic helmet with its DPM cover, the new style bergen with removable side pouches and '58 pattern belt order. He wears improved Northern Ireland body armour which is now worn under the latest pattern DPM combat dress. The weapon is the 5.56mm L24A1 also known as the 'SA80'. Note the CWS mounted on this weapon the SA80 was first issued to '42' early in 1986.

J3: Marine 'X' Company, 45 Commando, 1991

Marine Steve Drew is seen here during deployment on Operation Haven in northern Iraq during an attempt to provide a safe area for Kurdish refugees. At the time it was the largest RM deployment since the Falklands War. Marine Drew wears the windproof smock over temperate issue combat trousers. The belt order is the patter '90 PLCE and he is armed with L24A1 IW (individual weapon). Unit-purchased commercial chest pouch rigs were also issued in this unit.

Royal Marines fire the 81 mm L16 mortar during training on Ascension Island in 1982, prior to Operation Corporate on the Falkland Islands. The L16 can Wre 15 rounds per minute for indeWnite periods, and also be broken down into three loads which can be man packed. (W. Fowler)

K:

1: ORs beret badge, Kings Crown version.
2: Officers beret badge ERII version.
3: World War Two issue parachute wing.
4: Embroidered ROYAL MARINE flash with curved World War Two COMMANDO title and unit numbers.
5: RM Siege Regiment, grenade sleeve badge, World War Two.
6: Woven 'Cash tape' title with separate numbers, World War Two.
7: 34th Amphibious Support Regiment embroidered flash.
8: Royal Marine Engineers printed flash, World War Two.
9: 117 Royal Marine Brigade embroidered flash, 1945.

L:

1: Coloured shoulder strap loop 45 (RM) Cdo, 1944.
2: Combined operations flash, World War Two.
3: 30 Assault Unit flash, World War Two.
4: Embroidered 'ROYAL MARINE COMMANDO', 1946 to present day.
5: Embroidered or printed dagger flash.
6: Parachute wing tropical uniform.
7: Swimmer canoeist 1, Lovat Suit.
8: Kings Badge No.1 and Lovat Suit.
9: Royal Marine Sniper, Lovat Suit.
10: Parachute wing No.1 Dress.
11: Commandant General's shooting Badge 1990, Lovat Suit.

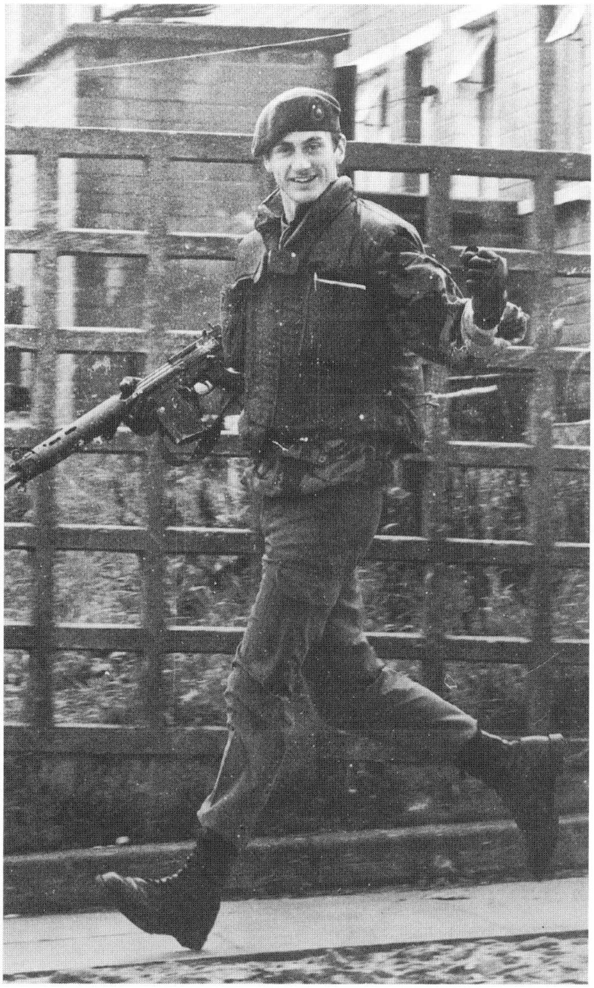

A cheerful Marine Commando of 45 Cdo RM on patrol in Belfast in September 1977. (W. Fowler)

Notes sur les planches en couleur

1 Porte l'uniforme de service 1902, modèle modifié distribué pour la première fois dans s années 20, une casquette souple de tranchées avec visière cousue et un équipement en ile modèle 1908 passé au blanco. Il est armé d'un SMLE No.1 Mk III.
2 Combinaison typique d'effets navals chauds utilisée par ces canonniers. Duffle coat ec capuche et gants anti-flammes et tenue de campagne bleue rentrée dans de lourdes ttes de mer en cuir.
3 Combinaison RN sous des gants et une capuche anti-flammes. Il porte le masque antiz modèle RN dans son boîtier et le casque d'acier est porté avec la mentonnière à l'arrière la tête.
1 Ce pilote porte une tenue de campagne kaki sous un gilet de sauvetage modèle 1932. Il ent son casque de pilote type B avec ses lunettes Mk III et son masque à oxygène type D. es bottes de pilote sont le modèle 1936.
2 Ce marine porte la veste de brousse KD à quatre poches et l'équipement en toile modèle 7 avec des bandes molletières courtes. Remarquez la barrette attachée autour des épaules, gilet de sauvetage d'assaut et deux bandoulières rondes en coton de munitions .303mm our son SMLE No.1 Mk III.
3 Encore une fois, battledress et équipement en toile modèle '37 avec barrette, coup-deing et couteau attaché à la ceinture. Il porte un masque en bandoulière et est armé d'une itraillette Thompson.
1 Porte tenue de campagne modèle '40 et sac à dos modèle '37 maintenu par des courroies '. Le badge de casquette n'était pas utilisé par cette unité et leur équipement en toile était uvent peint en motifs camouflage comme le sac à dos. Il porte le SMLE No. 4.
2 Ce marine, qui porte des cartouchières pour le canon Vickers 'K', porte l'uniforme odèle '37 et 50 bandoulières de coton rondes de cartouches .303 pour son SMLE No.4.
3 Ce marine, qui porte le peu apprécié 'Battle Jerkin' et le 'comforter' tricoté au lieu de n bérêt, est armé d'un MP 40 allemand capturé car son unité perdit la majorité de son

Farbtafeln

A1 Er trägt die 1902er Dienstkleidung im modifizierten Muster, wie sie erstmals in den 20er Jahren ausgegeben wurde, mit einer weichen Wettermütze mit abgestepptem Schirm und weiß gewachstem Gurtzeug. Er ist mit einer SMLE No.1 Nk III bewaffnet.
A2 Hier ist die typische Kombination der warmen Marineausrüstung abgebildet, die diese Schützenmannschaften trugen. Dufflecoat mit Anti-Flash-Kapuze und Handschuhen. Der blaue Kampfanzug wurde in schwere Marinestiefel aus Leder gesteckt.
A3 RN-Overall unter Anti-Flash-Handschuhen und Kapuze. Er hat das Gas-Atemschutzgerät in RN-Muster im Etui bei sich. Der Stahlhelm wird mit dem Kinnriemen nach hinten getragen.
B1 Der Pilot trägt einen khakifarbenen Kampfanzug unter der Schwimmweste in 1932er Muster. Er trägt seinen Fliegerhelm Typ B mit der MK 111-Schutzbrille und die Sauerstoffmask Typ D. Seine Fliegerstiefel entsprechen dem 1936er Modell.
B2 Dieser Marineinfanterist trägt die KD-Buschjacke mit vier Taschen und Gurtzeug im 1937er Muster mit Wickelgamaschen kurzen Stils. Man beachte die an den Schultern befestigte Knebelschnur, die Gefechtsschwimmweste und die beiden runden Schultergürtel aus Baumwolle, die 0,303mm Munition für seine SMLE No.1 Mk 111 enthalten.
B3 Kampfanzug und Gurtzeug wiederum im 1937er Muster mit Knebelschnur, Schlagring und Messer, die an Gürtel befestigt sind. Er hat ein Atemschutzgerät Umhängen und ist mit einer Thompson-Machinenpistole bewaffnet.
C1 Diese Figur trägt einen Kampfanzug iin 1940er Muster und einen Tornister Modell 1937, der mit "L"-Riemen befestigt ist. Diese Einheit trug keine Mützenabzeichen und ihr Gurtzeug war häufig – wie der Rucksack – in Tarnfarben angemalt. Er trägt ein SMLE No.4.
C2 Dieser Marineinfanterist trägt Trommelmagazine für das Vickers "K"-Gewehr und die 1937er Ausrüstung. Er hat 50 Runden-Gürtel aus Baumwolle bei sich mit 0,303mm-

matériel durant le débarquement.

D1 Ce béret bleu était adopté par les unités qui n'avaient pas le droit de porter le béret vert et également par les unités des opérations combinées en 1943. Le pantalon de combat modèle '37 avec pullover RN ajouté, les bretelles et la ceinture standard.

D2 Tenue de combat 'à parements' adoptée par les officiers avec les ailes de pilotes RN au dessus de la poche de poitrine gauche. Il porte le badge de casquette des officiers en deux parties sur son béret.

D3 Cet opérateur utilise la TSF No 38 introduite en 1943. Il porte l'insigne de l'unité d'assaut 30 et ses ailes de qualification de parachutiste sur les deux manches.

E1 Armé d'un SMG Thompson, ce NCO porte la tenue de combat vert et le pantalon vert jungle et divers matériels de l'armée américaine qu'il a acquis. Il a un sac à dos Burgen et des bandes molletières courtes introduites à partir de 1943.

E2 Ce marine, qui sert avec le 41 Cdo en Corée, prote l'uniforme de combat US M1943 standard, la cartouchière M1923 et est armé d'un fusil US MI Garand.

E3 Ce canonnier Bren porte une chemise angola, un pantalon B.D. en denim, des bandes molletières courtes, des bottes S.V. et un équipement en toile de modèle '37. Il porte les lunettes anti-gaz pour se protéger des tourbillons de sable.

F1 Cet officier porte le smock Denison sur la tenue de combat de 1946. Il a l'emblème 3 Cdo Bde d'un poignard et utilise leur technique de noircir sa ceinture de toile avec du cirage noir.

F2 On voit ici le Général Sir Ian Ritchie en chemise et pantalon tropicaux kaki, chaussures marron des officiers et une ceinture de corps.

F3 Chemise et short vert olive portés ici avec revers de chaussettes kaki, bandes molletières d'officier couleur pierre et les pompons blancs des porte-chaussettes du 42 Cdo.

G1 Chemise vert jungle, pantalon avec poche sur le côté et chapeau de brousse. Des bottes de jungle longues ou courtes auraient été utilisées. On voit également ici l'équipement en toile modèle '58 avec armature élastique auquel est attaché un grand paquetage modèle '58 et un sac de couchage roulé en poncho. Il est armé de l'armalite M16.

G2 Il porte le smock Denison sur un pantalon de combat en denim, des bandes molletières courtes et des bottes S.V. Il est armé du SL, introduit pour la première fois en 1959 dans le 3Cdo Bde.

G3 A cause du climat, ce marine porte une chemise K.G., un short remonté, des bandes molletières et des bottes S.V. L'équipement en toile modèle 1958 est utilisé avec un sac pour bouteille d'eau modèle '44.

H1 Gilet pare-balles US M69 porté sur une veste de combat vert olive. Il porte une ceinture modèle '58 avec cartouchière simple et son SLR conserve encore sa crosse en bois.

H2 Membre d'UNFICYP qui porte un 'woolly-pully' avec les titres de 'Royal Marine Command' ainsi qu'un badge bleu des Nations-Unies pour casquette et manches. Pantalon léger avec bandes molletières courtes et bottes DMS. Le SLR comporte maintenant une crosse en plastique noir.

H3 Porte une combinaison de vol verte avec gilet de sauvetage léger et gants de cuir noir privés.

I1 Matériel modèle 1958 avec un 'skid lid' suspendu par sa mentonnière au sac de sa main gauche. Il porte un pantalon léger avec de lourdes chaussures de marche civiles et des Chaussettes roulées. Il est armé d'un SMG Sterling 9mm.

I2 Le smock et le pantalon coupe-vent avec des bottes de parachutiste allemandes, acquisition privée, sont portés avec un équipement en toile de modèle '58 sans le 'bum roll' et avec un masque ajouté sur la gauche. Il est armé d'un SLR et d'un LAW de 66mm.

J1 Combinaison de cartouchière '58 et sacs WWII 'Bren' portés ensemble, avec une veste civile Nevispart Orion. Bergen modèle '58 avec tapis de couchage roulé sous le revers et pantalon DPM, chaussures de marche avec revers de chaussettes kaki.

J2 Casque ballistique Mk 6 avec housse DPM, bergen nouveau style avec sacs amovibles et ceinture modèle '58. Il porte le gilet pare-balles amélioré et est armé du SA80 5,56mm.

J3 Porte le smock coupe-vent par dessus le pantalon de combat standard. La ceinture est le modèle '90 PLCE et il est armé du SA80.

K1 Badge de béret O.R. version Kings Crown.

K2 Badge de béret d'officier version ER II.

K3 Aile parachute de la seconde guerre mondiale.

K4 Ecusson Royal Marine brodé avec titre WWII 'Commando' incurvé et numéros d'unité.

K5 Badge de manche RM Siege Regt Grenade WWII.

K6 Titre tissé 'Cash Tape' avec numéros séparés, WWII.

K7 Ecusson brodé du 34ème régiment amphibien de soutien.

K8 Ecusson imprimé des ingénieurs Rm, WWII.

K9 Ecusson brodé du 117 RM Bde, 1945.

L1 Boucle d'épaulette colorée, 45 (RM) Cdo 1944.

L2 Ecusson des opérations combinées, WWII.

L3 Flast de la 30 Assault Unit, WWII.

L4 'Royal Marine Commando' brodé de 1946 à nos jours.

L5 Ecusson poignard brodé ou imprimé.

L6 Uniforme tropical de l'aile parachutisme.

L7 Lovat Suit de nageur/canoë.

L8 Badge du roi, No. 1 et Lovat Suit.

L9 Tireur Royal Marine, Lovat Suit.

L10 Aile parachutiste, uniforme No. 1.

L11 Badge de tir du Commandant Général, 1990 Lovat Suit.

Patronen für seine SMLE No.4.

C3 Dieser Marineinfanterist trägt das unbeliebte "Kampfwams" und einen gestrickten "Schal" anstelle saines Baretts und ist mit einer eingenommenen deutschen MP40 bewaffnet, da ein Großteil der Ausrüstung seiner Einheit bei der Truppenlandung verlorenging.

D1 Das blaue Barett wurde von Einheiten getragen, die eigentlich nicht dazu berechtigt waren, das grüne zu tragen, sowie von denjenigen, die im Verlauf von 1943 an gemeinsamen Einsätzen teilnahmen. Hier sind die Hosen des Kampfanzuges in 1937er Muster mit zusätzlichem RN-Pullover, ausgegebenen Hosenträgern und der Korps-Koppel.

D2 Er trägt den Kampfanzug "mit Aufschlägen" der Offiziere mit den RN-Fliegerabzeichen über der linken Brusttasche. Auf dem Barett sieht man das zweiteilige Mützenabzeichen der Offiziere.

D3 Dieser Funker bedient das 1943 eingeführte Funkgerät No-38 und trägt das Abzeichen der 30. Gefechtseinheit sowie sein Fallschirmspringerabzeichen auf beiden Ärmeln.

E1 Dieser Unteroffizier ist mit einer Thompson-Maschinenpistole bewaffnet und trägt die dschungelgrüne Kampfjacke, Hosen und verschiedene Ausrüstungsteile, die aus der Ausgabe der amerikanischen Armee stammen und deren er habhaft wurde. Er hat einen Bergen-Rucksack und die 1943 eingeführte kurzen Wickelgamaschen.

E2 Dieser Marineinfanterist dient im 41. Kommando in Korea und trägt die Standard-Kampfkleidung US M1943, den Patronengürtel M1923 und ist mit dem US MI Garand-Gewehr bewaffnet.

E3 Dieser Bren-Schütze trägt ein Angola-Hemd, B.D.-Hosen aus Denim, kurze Wickelgamaschen, S.V.-Stiefel und 1937er Gurtzeug. Die Gasschutzbrille wird als Schutz gegen aufliegenden Sand getragen.

F1 Dieser Offizier trägt den Kampfanzug im 194aer Muster. Er trägt das Dolch-Emblem der 3. Kommando-Brigade und weist ihr Kennzeichen der Textilkoppel auf, die mit Schuhwachs schwarz eingefärbt wurde.

F2 General Sir Ian Ritchie ist hier mit khakifarbenem Tropenhemd, Hosen mit brauner Offiziersschuhen und einer Korpskoppel abgebildet.

F3 Hier sind olivgrüne Hosen und Shorts mit khakifarbenen Strümpfen abgebildet, steinfarbenen Wickelgamaschen der Offiziere und den weißen Strumpfpatten des 42. Kommandos.

G1 Dschungelgrünes Hemd, Hosen mit Seitentasche und Buschhelm. Wahrscheinlich trug man Dschungelstiefel in kurzer oder langer Machart. Ebenso sieht man das Gurtzeug im 58er Muster mit einem Tragegestell, auf dem das große Packstück im 58er Muster und der Schlafsack, der in einen Poncho gerollt wurde, festgeschnallt wurde. Er ist mit einem M16-Gewehr bewaffnet.

G2 Er trägt den Denison-Kittel über Kampfhosen aus Denim, kurze Wickelgamaschen und S.V.-Stiefel. Er ist mit der SLR bewaffnet, die 1959 erstmals bei der 3. Kommando-Brigade eingeführt wurde.

G3 Aufgrund der klimatischen Verhältnisse trägt dieser Marineinfanterist ein K.D.-Hemd, aufgerollte Shorts Wickelgamaschen und S.V.-Stiefel. Das 1958er Gurtzeug wird mit einem Feldflaschenbeutel des 1944er Musters verwendet.

H1 US M69-Körperpanzer wird über der olivgrünen Kampfjacke getragen. Er trägt den Gürtel des 1958er Musters mit einem einzelnen Patronenetui. Die SLR, die er bei sich hat, hat noch den hölzernen Schaft.

H2 Mitglied der UNFICYP im "Woolly-Pully" mit der Aufschrift "Royal Marine Command" und der blauen UN-Mütze und Ärmelabzeichen. Die leichten Hosen werden mit kurzen Wickelgamaschen und DMS-Stiefeln getragen. Die SLR hat inzwischen einen schwarzen Kunststoff-Schaft.

H3 Diese Figur trägt einen grünen Fliegeranzug mit leichter Schwimmweste und privat erworbenen schwarzen Lederhandschuhen.

I1 Hier trägt man die Ausrüstung des 1958er Musters, der Sturzhelm ist an seinem Kinnriemen am linken Beutel aufgehängt. Er trägt leichte Hosen mit schweren, zivilen Wanderschuhen und aufgerollten Strümpfen. Er ist mit einer 9mm Sterling-Maschinenpistole bewaffnet.

I2 Hier ist der windfeste Kittel und die Hosen mit deutschen Fallschirmspringerstiefeln, die privat erworben wurden, mit dem Gurtzeug im 1958er Muster ohne die "hintere Packrolle" und einem Atemschutzgerät an der linken Seite kombiniert. Er ist mit einer SLR und einer 66mm LAW bewaffnet.

J1 Kombination eines 58er Magazins und der "Bren"-Beutel aus dem Zweiten Weltkrieg hier zusammen mit einer zivilen Nevispart Orion-Jacke. Bergen-Rucksack im SAS-Muster mit dem aufgerollten Schlafmatte unter der Klappe, DPN-Hosen, Wanderstiefel und khakifarbene strü'mpfe.

J2 Mk 6 ballistischer Helm mit DPM-Helmbezug, Bergen-Rucksack im neuen Stil mit abnehmbaren Taschen und 58er Gürtel. Er trägt den verbesserten Körperpanzer und ist mit der 5,56mm SA80 bewaffnet.

J3 Diese Figur trägt den windfesten Kittel über den ausgegebenen Kampfhosen. Die Koppel entspricht dem 90er Muster PLCE, und er ist mit der SA80 bewaffnet.

K1 O.R.-Barettabzeichen in der Version Kings Crown.

K2 Barettabzeichen der Offiziere in der Version ER 11.

K3 Fallschirmspringerabzeichen wie im Zweiten Weltkrieg ausgegeben.

K4 Gesticktes Abzeichen des Royal Marine mit geschwungenem "Kommando"-Titel des Zweiten Weltkriegs und Nummer der Einheit.

K5 Armelabzeichen des Siege Regiment Grenade aus dem Zweiten Weltkrieg.

K6 Gewobene "Cash Tape"-Aufschrift mit separaten Nummern aus dem Zweiten Weltkrieg.

K7 Gesticktes Abzeichen des 34th Amphibious Support Regiment.

K8 Gedrucktes Abzeichen der RM Engineers aus dem Zweiten Weltkrieg.

K9 Gesticktes Abzeichen des 117 RM Brigade, 1945.

L1 Farbiges Schulterklappen-Band, 45 (Rm) Kommando 1944.

L2 Abzeichen der gemeinsamen Einsätze aus dem Zweiten Weltkrieg.

L3 Abzeichen der 30 Assault Unit aus dem Zweiten Weltkrieg.

L4 Gesticktes Abzeichen "IRoyal Marine Commando" von 1946 bis zur Gegenwart.

L5 Gesticktes beziehungsweise gedrucktes Dolch-Abzeichen.

L6 Fallschirmspringerabzeichen auf Tropenuniform.

L7 Schwimmer/Kanufahrer, 1. Lovat Suit.

L8 King's-Abzeichen, No. 1 und Lovat Suit.

L9 Heckenschütze der Royal Marine, Lovat Suit.

L10 Fallschirmspringerabzeichen, No. 1 Anzug.

L11 Schießabzeichen des Commandant General, Lovat Suit 1990.